dixi
boo

D1333818

Joe Gray

Joe Gray is a field naturalist who lives in the catchment of the River Colne on the island known as Great Britain. He has a master's degree in Zoology from Cambridge and another in Forestry from Bangor, and he is a Fellow of the Royal Entomological Society. Joe is also a co-founder of *The Ecological Citizen* (a peer-reviewed, nature-centred journal), a Knowledge Advisor on ecological ethics for the United Nations' Harmony with Nature programme, and Chair of GENIE (the Global Ecocentric Network for Implementing Ecodemocracy).

As a trustee and volunteer naturalist at Highfield Park—his local charity-run green space—he leads courses for people of all ages on various aspects of natural history and reconnecting with nature. He is also an Associate Tutor on the Field Studies Council's extensive nature-learning programme. Other teaching activities in which he has been involved include the delivery of sessions to British and international secondary-school students on the rights of nature.

Joe spends much of his spare time, when not in 'lockdown', wandering the surviving scraps of wild nature within the industrialized landscape that surrounds his home. He also writes fiction under the pen name Dewey Dabbar.

Thirteen Paces by Four:
Backyard Biophilia and the Emerging Earth Ethic

—————◇—————

Joe Gray

Dixi Books
Copyright © 2021 by Joe Gray
Copyright © 2021 Dixi Books
All rights reserved. No part of this book may be used or reproduced or transmitted to any form or by any means, electronic or mechanical, including photocopying, recording, or by any information and retrieval system, without written permission from the Publisher.

Thirteen Paces by Four: Backyard Biophilia and the Emerging Earth Ethic
Joe Gray
Editor: Katherine Boyle
Proofreading: Andrea Bailey
Designer: Pablo Ulyanov
I. Edition: January 2021

Library of Congress Cataloging-in Publication Data
Joe Gray - 1st ed.
ISBN-13: 978-1-913680-06-0
1. Ecology. 2. Adult Non-Fiction. 3. Natural History. 4. Sustainability.
5. Environmental Conservation. 6. Nature Writing.
7. Wildlife Gardening. 8. Urban Ecology.

This book is printed on sustainably sourced paper.

© Dixi Books Publishing
293 Green Lanes, Palmers Green,
London, England
N13 4XS
info@dixibooks.com
www.dixibooks.com

Thirteen Paces by Four:
Backyard Biophilia and the Emerging Earth Ethic

———◇———

Joe Gray

dixi
books

The Voice of the New Age

100% of the royalties from this book will
be donated to the **World Land Trust**

For colour versions of the photos in this book, please visit
https://dixibooks.com/categories/ecology/thirteen-paces-by-four/
or use the short URL https://is.gd/13paces

Contents

*To the plants, insects, and other
creatures with whom I share a home place*

And to Trevor, who taught me a good deal about them

Foreword

South Dublin Libraries
www.southdublinlibraries.ie

With *Thirteen Paces by Four*, Joe Gray has written a new classic of ecological literature. In its own unassuming way, it stands alongside the work of Aldo Leopold, Edward Abbey, John Muir, Annie Dillard and others in the same class—but especially, perhaps, that of Henry David Thoreau. Because what Gray does is to find and follow wildness, famously described by Thoreau as the preservation of the world, starting not in a wilderness but a garden.

From there we find ourselves, before long, in wild-flower meadows, the wildwood and its surviving successors, rivers, and sunlight, and among all manner of creatures, from insects and amphibians to birds and mammals, all described with loving attention to detail. Finally, we arrive at the Earth itself, whence there is nowhere else, let alone better, to go.

In a parallel way, working out from the challenges and opportunities of gardening, Gray uncovers the most important kinds of human relationships with the rest of the natural world. With originality and subtlety, he describes both the differences and the mutuality of a primal emotional love of nature ('biophilia') and a disinterested recognition of the intrinsic value of nature, its moral standing independently of its usefulness for us ('ecocentrism'). In the process, the bankruptcy of our ruling instrumentalism is quietly and effectively revealed. 'Necrocentrism' operates under the banner of unstoppable progress, but it is actually driven by fear, ignorance, and greed.

In the end, we return to the now deep-green neighbourhood, more aware that in all our lives and situations as Earthlings, even the most humble or straitened, more-than-human nature—including ourselves as natural beings—is never absent or irrelevant. The fact that we are Earthlings is finally the most important one of all. So what could be more important than waking up to that fact, respecting and even revering it, and deciding to work intelligently with it?

Rampant urbanization does not invalidate that lesson; it makes it more urgent. Absorbing it might also help us finally to face up (as Gray does) to the utter irresponsibility of human overpopulation.

The choice is already upon us. It is between human self-limitation, on the one hand, and ecocidal collapse, including of ourselves, on the other. With insight, compassion, and humour, Gray's fine book moves us in the direction of sanity and sanctity. I take my organic cotton hat off to him.

— *Patrick Curry*

Preface

The writing of this book began with a handshake in a Turkish café near Piccadilly Circus. The hand that I shook was that of my contact at Dixi Books, and, as it happens, she was the last person whom I would greet in this way for many months. Soon, social-distancing measures were introduced across Britain as part of efforts to slow the spread of Covid-19. With these measures, the idea that I had pitched that day—over a smoky black filter coffee—rapidly became unworkable. (Meanwhile, to keep my eye in, I practised my handshake with my wife.)

The book that I proposed was going to be inspired by several trips that I had on the horizon. These included short youth-hostelling breaks in the New Forest and South Downs National Parks, a fortnight's immersion in what remains of the once-vast Caledonian Forest, and rail journeys to unspoilt wildlife havens in rural France and Spain. That, of course, was not how things panned out.

It is remarkable how the extinguishing of liberties, or just the threat of such a thing, can so sharply crystallize what one values most in life. An example will illustrate this. One wet and wintry afternoon, when I was nineteen years old and at university, I injured my back in a football match. I was strapped onto a stretcher by paramedics and taken to a hospital that was already brimming with people in mud-caked sports kits who, between them, were clutching the gamut of body parts. It was, in other words, a typical Saturday. I had a torturous wait in a hospital bed for my turn to be wheeled into the X-ray room so that the extent of the injury could be determined; and all the while I had to remain motionless, in order to avoid risking exacerbation of the as-yet undiagnosed problem. During that inanimate wait, there was one particular concern that weighed heavily on me. The worry was that I might never again be able to climb a mountain or leap from rock to rock under a waterfall.

Up to that point in my life, I had not realized just how important this manifestation of independence was to me. Thus, when I was informed that the damage was muscular only and would slowly heal with rest (two decades on, it is almost there), I vowed to never take for granted the liberty to explore wild places. And on no occasion have I. With every day spent among nature's biological and geological wonders, I grow more grateful still.

In the case of the escalation of social restrictions during the early phase of the Covid-19 pandemic, the spectre of two potential lost liberties pressed most forcibly on me. The first was the ability to buy good food, by which I mean raw ingredients and artisan products that are organic, minimally packaged, and locally sourced where possible. For preserving this freedom for me, I express sincere gratitude to the staff of several small shops—especially B Healthy, the Green Kitchen, and the Refill Pantry—along with the Brown Bread market stall, all of which are walkable from my home in the small English city of St Albans. (Readers with a passion for the history of organic produce may be interested to learn that Heath & Heather, a century-old purveyor of close-to-nature teas, was founded by a St Albans seed merchant named Samuel Ryder—along with his brother James—and had their first premises just down the hill, as it happens, from the Refill Pantry.)

The second thing that I feared losing was the freedom to walk around the woodland and grassland near my home, marvelling at the wild flowers and trees, and the birds, bugs, and bees—let's call it 'exercise' for the sake of putting a name on it. It is appropriate here to offer a further expression of thanks, and that is to the Verulam Golf

Club for opening their private eighteen-hole course to locals who were seeking a large area of uncrowded green space. I took regular advantage of the opportunity that this provided for walking in the shadows of majestic ancient oaks (see Figure 0.1), ambling under flower-rich banks, and strolling along a stunning stretch of the Ver chalk stream—taking in sights, smells, and sounds that are otherwise off-limits. (Readers with a passion for the history of golf may be interested to learn that this is the course that sparked a fondness for the game in a St Albans seed merchant named Samuel Ryder—yes, the same one—who would go on to donate the trophy for a certain biennial transatlantic tournament.)

Figure 0.1: A huge ancient oak tree on Verulam Golf Course.

At the same time as I was fretting about the precariousness of the freedom to roam woodland and grassland, I was growing a new appreciation for having a backyard. For even if the army started patrolling my street, no one would be able to stop me opening up the French windows in my kitchen and stepping out into the rear garden. And thus we reach the setting for the book that you have here, the one I ended up writing.

There are people lucky enough to have large gardens, and even a wood or a meadow, within their property. I am not one of those people. My own present fortune—beyond living without fear of oppression, poverty, homelessness, famine, severe drought, or war— lies instead in the conveniences afforded by residing in a small city, such as good public transport links. My back garden, as is celebrated in the title of this book, measures just thirteen paces by four.

But, wait. What am I doing when I call this parcel of the Earth's surface 'mine', as in 'my back garden'? Here, as all too often, habits of talk conceal important blind spots. There might be a legal document that assigns the garden to me, but the type of ownership thus granted is one that rudely ignores other-than-human interests. So, to be clear, when in this book I call the land 'my' garden—or (where it better suits the context) 'our' garden, meaning that of Romita, my wife, too—I do so only as a shorthand. For the garden is an area of land that we cohabit with many other beings.

Returning to the discussion of the back garden's dimensions, it is not an area of land that, based on human perceptions, could be described as large. During the restrictions on movement relating to the pandemic, however, even the smallest of gardens has proved a mercy, as compared with having no garden at all. I have colleagues who live in blocks of flats with either a single small patch of nectarless grass that is shared between many residents or, worse, no communal green space at all. One such individual told me how she got extraordinarily excited when a peacock butterfly settled for a short while on the window of her upper-floor flat. And rightly so.

I should be clear at this point that while Covid-19 has funnelled the focus of the narrative to my back garden, this is not a book about the pandemic and its powerful reminder of our place in nature. I have sufficient experience in the humdrum work of medical editing—the part-time vocation that puts a shirt on my back, if not a spring in my step—to know that this is a topic for me to avoid. And, in any case, it is largely unclear, at the time of writing, how the pathogen's natural history is going to unfold. Thus, Covid-19 will, outside of the Preface, feature as just brief mentions here and there, where its impacts (such as the quieter skies and a waning choice of coffee beans) are directly relevant. Nor will I dwell on the topics of confinement or lost liberties.

Rather, I will leave the books on Covid-19 to others. Possible titles to consider include *A New Pavement Etiquette: The Cyclists' Omnipotence and the Death of Thank Yous,* or *The Greens Were Right All Along: Society Can Change Rapidly,* or *Judgement Day: How the Social Police Despise Pandemic Spreaders but Overlook Air Polluters and Tolerate Water Wasters.* Okay, that last one, in particular, might need some wordsmithing, but you get the idea. (I will retreat into parentheses to offer one more possible title: *Do-It-Yourself Dentistry.* This suggestion is inspired by my dad's decision, during 'lockdown', to pull out his own tooth rather than troubling a dentist with his presence. This is a rather extreme case of the stereotypically British behaviour of not wanting to burden health professionals with one's troubles. Of course, other than the saving of petrol from him not having to make a ten-mile round trip, this is irrelevant to a book that has an environmental theme, but I did think it deserved to be recorded somewhere. And, as a qualifier, I should add that, while the act was certainly heroic, I have a suspicion that it was in part motivated by him having run out of odd jobs to do around the house and craving something else on which he could use his pliers.)

I admit to an envy of the ready access to large, non-urbanized areas that has helped inspire many of the great nature writers of the Western world. Henry Thoreau, famously, had the woods around the cabin he built near the edge of Walden Pond. Jean-Henri Fabre visited numerous sites in the western Provence countryside for his pioneering observations in entomology (the study of insects). John Muir—to note just one of his many fonts of mental stimulation—drew on the glory of Yosemite Valley. Mary Austin had the Mojave Desert to inspire her *Land of Little Rain*. Aldo Leopold found meaning in his biotically rich farm on the south bank of the Wisconsin River, his 'Sand County', where much of the philosophical dreaming that led to the land ethic happened (I will elaborate on this in Chapter 4). Nan Shepherd, author of the acclaimed *Living Mountain*, resided in the figurative shadow of the Cairngorms. And Ed Abbey benefitted from most of non-tarmacked Utah and Arizona. That is just a sample. (Please note that I am about to start a new paragraph. That is because I do not wish to dishonour such luminaries by discussing my own writing in the same section of unbroken prose as theirs.)

Before I started on the present book, I had thought that if ever I was going to do justice to the heritage of the great nature writers, my chance would lie in an abandoned village in depopulated rural Spain or some forgotten inland valley in southern France (there was one such valley that I had in mind when I spoke with my contact at Dixi Books in the café near Piccadilly Circus). But maybe the enforced shift in focus to a minuscule urban locality was a blessing. I am aware that those who have lost loved ones to the pandemic will not necessarily be so quick to find silver linings, but I use the word 'blessing' with good reason. For one thing, I am a champion of the appreciation of local nature (although I admit that focusing on a small back garden takes this to an extreme level). For another, as the bounds of my wanderings are so much more confined than those of Thoreau *et al.*, I feel entitled to some leniency in my quest to avoid disgracing the tradition. For a third, I can write this book safe in the knowledge that the study of a backyard is one of the two intellectual pursuits for which no one can fairly be branded a dilettante. (The other, a subject on which I add nothing of note in the present work, is the back of one's hand.)

I must point out that finding inspiration for nature writing within the confines of a single garden is not new. Jennifer Owen, in perhaps the best-known example, wrote books that marked the fifteen- and thirty-year points in her astonishing audit of a tiny patch of suburban Leicester. (I say 'tiny' but note that I could comfortably fit a dozen or more of my back gardens into her 741 square metres.) In her long-term study, which began in 1972, Owen recorded well over two thousand species, including several parasitic wasps that were new to science. What made her achievement all the more remarkable was that for a large part of it she was living with multiple sclerosis. My intention here, though, is somewhat different from an exercise in exhaustive cataloguing. Instead, while I will be introducing you to a number of life forms that make a home in, or otherwise visit, the garden, I intend to go beyond the realm of natural history.

It will not all be happy reading, and so, in Part One, I begin with a chapter on eco-psychology. Next comes a discussion of the history of the landscape where I live. And only with those two topics explored do I then invite you into the garden itself, in Chapter 3. Parts Two and Three examine a number of facets of life in the garden that illustrate the manifestations of biophilia—the powerful affinity that humans have with the more-than-human world—and the implications of an Earth ethic, in which non-human nature is granted moral standing. Finally, Part Four comprises a single short chapter in which I worry about the future of the garden and life on Earth more generally.

Given the particularly small nature of my back garden and the rather ambitious scope of the topic matter, I hope that you, the reader, will forgive my intermittent mental forays outside the rectangle of thirteen paces by four.

—◇—◇—◇—

I will finish this brief preface with some acknowledgements, some comments on referencing, and finally an observation on anthropomorphisms.

Acknowledgements
First, I am grateful to Dixi Books for giving me this opportunity to write on a topic for which I have deep passion.

Secondly, I am indebted to other proponents of Earth-centred thinking. These include Adam Dickerson, Eileen Crist, Ian Whyte, Patrick Curry, and other fellow editors and advisors on *The Ecological Citizen*, as well as Alf and Tasha Seegert, Simon Leadbeater, and Helen Kopnina, among many more people, not least those who are part of the GENIE ecodemocracy project. Here I will also offer thanks to the numerous ecologists, including Chris Gibson and Ian Carle, who, through their combination of immense knowledge and a willingness to speak up, help give non-humans a voice. Chris is as vociferous and passionate a champion as wildlife could ever hope to have, while Ian does sterling work ensuring that the 'underappreciated majority'—the invertebrates—do not get overlooked.

All of these people ensure that I do not feel "alone in a world of wounds." I should also note that Adam, Ian, and Patrick, along with Chris and his wife Jude, each provided critical comment on a draft of this book, which was a most generous undertaking on their part, and one that, in different ways, significantly enhanced the final product (errors, though, are mine alone).

Thirdly, for his help on the history of Fleetville, the suburb of St Albans in which the garden is sited, as well as his habit of sharing other fascinating titbits, gratitude is owed to David Gaylard.

Fourthly, I must express thanks to Richard Mabey, whose book *Weeds* I read with great pleasure as I wrote the early chapters of the present work and have drawn on in a number of places.

Fifthly, I must, of course, thank my wife, who is one of many cohabiters of the garden (I am available for writing wedding vows, should you have a need).

Lastly, I will remain ever grateful to all the naturalists with whom I have spent time in the field. If I had not, for instance, had the good fortune to meet William Bishop, my knowledge of botany would be pitiful rather than merely passable. And there are many other people who have been generous in sharing with me their knowledge and love of the world around them.

This last bunch includes the truly remarkable Trevor James, who helped me unlock so much of the joy that I get from the world around me. Trevor, the most patient teacher I have known, passed away during the writing of this book after a long and spirited battle against cancer. He was buried wearing his floppy hat and holding a field notebook and hand lens (just as any self-respecting naturalist should be, when the time comes—for you never know when you might need them).

A note on referencing

In order to keep the prose as aesthetically clean as possible (it is cluttered up enough as it is, on account of my predilection for parenthetical asides), I have not cited sources within the main body of the text. However, there is a fair-sized bibliography at the end of the book where supporting materials for each chapter are presented, organized by author surname. So where I have quoted someone or otherwise referred to their work, please do have a look in the bibliography if you are interested in finding out more about the specific source.

A note on 'anthropomorphisms'

To some readers, it may seem that when, for instance, I state that a plant *wants* something, I am 'anthropomorphizing' nature (i.e. attributing exclusively human characteristics and behaviours to non-humans). But I would (politely) reject this idea. Those traits that many among us like to claim as distinctively human are in fact much more broadly shared. New research and observations continue to reinforce this point. Furthermore, since the English language has evolved to describe the world in human terms, it is thus inadequate for fully expressing the subtle workings of agency and interests across the spectrum of non-human lives. So when, to repeat the above example, I say that a plant wants something, rest assured that the word has not been chosen lazily but instead reflects a conscious desire, working within the limited bounds of today's English, to reflect that the plant has interests. ●

Part one

Introduction

Chapter 1: Braving the storm of now

Floating down a river
Swinging through the trees
Climbing up a mountain
Going with the breeze
All of us can have a happy healthy place to be
If we can float and swim and climb in Earthling harmony
We are all Earthlings
We are all Earthlings
Spinning around together
On a planet of the Sun

— Lyrics from the Sesame Street song *We Are All Earthlings* (1990)

I am undergoing a metamorphosis, and it takes place as I walk in the mountains, as I canoe down a river, and as I sit out in my back garden. In every such moment of contact with the wider natural world, I am becoming a little less only-human and a little more Earthling.

While I have a penchant for science fiction novels, especially those like *The Disestablishment of Paradise* that say something important about humans' abuse of other life forms, it is not this that has inspired my choice of the word 'Earthling' in the first paragraph of the opening chapter of this book. Rather, the term expresses the increasing sense of solidarity that I have with all life—a oneness that goes far beyond the members of my family, the fellow human inhabitants of my bioregion, and all others in my species—and also captures the increasingly deep feeling of care that goes with it.

I use the term 'Earthling', also, in deference to Stan Rowe—a brilliant ecological philosopher who described himself in such a way and wrote, in *Earth Alive*, that we "are Earthlings first, humans second." Following Rowe's habits, I give 'Earthling' and 'Earth' an initial capital. After all, what could be more important than our one shared home?

My own journey to Earthlingness will complete itself when I return to the soil (through a green burial, assuming that the will which I have made survives as long as I do). The blossoming of Earthlingness between now and then, powered as it is by my living within a more-than-human world, will largely be out of my control. That is not to say that I lack the ability to stifle its development. This is something that I could no doubt achieve by splitting my time between air-conditioned offices, urban roads, indoor shopping centres, and a hermetically sealed home, and thus eliminating contact with most living nature. (And how convenient my self-closeting within such human artefacts would be for those powers that seek ever-more infrastructural growth by furthering the destruction of nature without impediment.) But I am not going to take this approach. For to do so would be to cauterize the large majority of life's meaning and significance. And it would also mean depriving myself of so many other beings to love, to coexist with, to look out for, and to revere.

Grasping the significance of non-human life through a bond of solidarity and care, I must stress, is something that comes with a price. The cost is that it exposes oneself to an increased magnitude of mental pain wherever there is harm. In that respect, though, it is no different from revering and loving, as opposed to merely liking, a fellow human—an undertaking that amplifies both the sorrow and the joy that arise from the relationship.

And just as there is a cost to such solidarity and caring, there is a price attached to the knowledge of life's fate. This idea was well expressed by Aldo Leopold, in a reflective essay within the posthumously published collection *Round River*, when he wrote that a penalty of "an ecological education is that one lives alone in a world of wounds."

Knowing too much and caring without bounds—these two things, for a human Earthling, are intertwined and inseparable.

There are several types of mental pain resulting specifically from harm to the more-than-human world that have been defined, with environmental philosopher Glenn Albrecht being a pioneer in their study. Albrecht's outputs include, in addition to the customary suite of academic papers, a recent summation of his work in the book *Earth Emotions*. In this, he describes how his contributions to eco-psychology began with the conception of 'solastalgia', which he defines as "the lived experience of distressing, negative environmental change." From this starting point he developed the umbrella term 'psychoterratic' to cover the varied emotional and psychological experiences that arise from living within nature, of which solastalgia is just one. This, in turn, gave rise to his 'psychoterratic typology', in which he draws his own ideas together with those of fellow contributors to the field of eco-psychology.

Before I dig deeper into the work of Albrecht, I will issue the cautionary note that it will not appeal to all. For some people, it might just seem like an attempt by the academic world to take possession of an important part of human experience, using inelegant labels to unsubtly describe things that are already, and much more richly, expressed in art, poetry, and religious traditions. For my present purpose, though, I do find it helpful to have single-word terms to put to concepts that I wish to explore, and I am grateful for Albrecht's organizing work.

With that said, I will now return to the psychoterratic states listed in the typology. Besides solastalgia, these include 'eco-anxiety', which is the deep concern that arises from experience or knowledge of negative ecological changes, and 'eco-paralysis', which is the perceived inability to do anything to help given the scale of the problems. Importantly, the typology embraces not just negative mental phenomena but positive ones too. The two broad kinds of phenomena, Albrecht contends in *Earth Emotions*, "are in lockstep, as you cannot have one without the other."

Albrecht's eco-psychological synthesis is a work in progress, both in the breadth of phenomena that it covers and in the way that overlapping concepts are delineated, but even in a nascent form it has utility, I feel, in concisely expressing the varied ways in which people may respond to the wider world around them. To give a personal example, I find that 'eutierria', one of the positive emotional states, helps describe my feeling of Earthlingness, which I related at the beginning of this chapter. Eutierria is the feeling of oneness and connectedness that arises when the boundaries break down between oneself and the more-than-human world.

I also find the concepts within the typology to be useful in helping me describe my own mental reactions to the homogenization and draining of life's essence by industrialized human societies. As such, I wish that I could have called this opening chapter something like 'A primer on overcoming eco-anxiety' or 'Say goodbye to solastalgia for good'. The problem with these titles is that they would falsely imply that I can suggest cures and that I have a way to break the 'lockstep' of negative and positive.

Instead, in this book, I am going to be advocating a philosophy that exposes its proponents to many additional sources of dread, anguish, and mental pain. (I am still perfecting the sales pitch.) What I am talking about is the emerging Earth ethic in which non-human nature is granted moral standing. This can be termed the 'deep green worldview', where the adjective 'deep' signifies that the philosophy's sphere of interest extends well beyond 'shallow', human-only concerns (such as 'resource depletion') to also encompass concerns for the flourishing of the non-human world that are independent of any associated benefits for humans. For the helpful distinction between 'shallow' and 'deep', in this context, we have the Norwegian philosopher Arne Næss to thank.

I will save expounding the contrast between shallow and deep concerns until my main treatment of the topic, which comes in Chapter 4. For now, I will just present a couple of examples that shed light on the difference and that have a direct relevance to the topic of negative psychoterratic states.

The first example is a generic and brief one and concerns rising sea levels, which are one possible trigger of eco-anxiety. Shallow concerns (a slightly unfortunate term, in the context) might be that flooding will hamper human flourishing through the sea's swallowing of inhabited islands. Deep concerns would consider negative impacts on humans but also encompass the loss of habitat for other life forms, including on islands not populated by *Homo sapiens*. The shallow concerns are a real and legitimate cause for eco-anxiety, but the deep concerns are, in a sense, immeasurably greater.

The second example, which combines two related cases, is one that is personal to me and lengthier. To explain the context for the example, I should first note that I spend much of my spare time roaming landscapes that are neither purely urban nor purely countryside. The environmental and social campaigner Marion Shoard has labelled these hybrid landscapes the 'edgelands' and describes them thus:

> Characterised by an anarchic mix of unloved land-use functions ranging from gravel workings to sewage disposal plants set in a scruffy mixture of unkempt fields, derelict industrial plant and miscellaneous wasteland [...] it is a refuge for wildlife driven out of an increasingly inhospitable countryside; it is a living museum of the workings of contemporary society; and it has considerable, untapped recreational potential.

One such edgeland is an old grassy aerodrome near my home in St Albans, where the de Havilland DH 106 Comet, the world's first commercial jet airliner, was developed and manufactured. The airfield closed in 1994 and in the following few years it was used for shooting scenes for a World War II film, *Saving Private Ryan*, and a similarly themed television series titled *Band of Brothers*. Around this time, government documents began to emerge that contained contradictory statements on the future of the site. Depending on which section you looked at, you could be left thinking that much of the area would become a country park or community woodland, or that it would be turned into a huge quarry for gravel extraction. In reality, it seems that the plan was always to quarry as much of the site as possible and then create the country park several decades later. Since green space for wildlife and recreation was supposed to be factored into the airfield's future, so as to 'compensate' for the development of some infrastructure on the site, one could be forgiven for thinking of the proverb about trying to eat cake and keep it too.

In the interim, while the old aerodrome's fate is decided, the area has been opened up for recreational use, including by walkers and bird watchers. A particular attraction for the latter group is that, as scrubby grassland, the place is important both as a summer breeding site for warblers and as a transit area for migrating birds refuelling during their long journeys.

As a local resident, I had the difficult choice of whether to get to know the place intimately or not. I felt that a future loss of access, if I did get attached to the site, would not cause me too much anguish from a shallow, recreational perspective, as I could easily find other places for walking. In contrast, I knew that becoming intertwined with the interests of the wildlife—in other words, developing deep concerns—is something that would expose me to the risk of a powerful solastalgia when quarrying began.

At this point, I will venture into a brief and more general discussion of perceived replaceability in this context. The idea that two places as instances of general traits—sources of recreation, say— are interchangeable helps grease the wheels of such notions as biodiversity 'offsetting'. In the ideology of offsetting, the tarmacking-over of a woodland can be justified if an equivalent area of trees is planted elsewhere, while a pond can be filled in as long as a similar-sized hole in the ground is dug up in another spot. The perception of replaceability ignores the *genius loci*, or pervading spirit, of individual places. And to the amphibians returning, out of hard-wired habit, to their breeding site, only to find that it has vanished, the presence of a new pond elsewhere provides no compensation at all.

Relatedly, to a person who has a deep love of a place, its destruction is in no way compensated for by the 'creation' of something similar in a different location. Indeed, part of my motivation for writing a whole book, here, about a tiny parcel of land is that knowing a place deeply, in its unique particularity, is part of reverencing the Earth: it both expresses this love and helps fuel it.

In regard to the example of the old grassy aerodrome that I presented above, the decision that I made—after responding as passionately as I could to the consultation on the place's future—was to spend my time getting to know a nearby site instead. This other site, I reckoned, faced a much lower risk of negative environmental change. And if ever there was archetypal edgeland, this place was surely it. From what I can work out about this other site's post-agricultural history, it was first quarried for gravel and then used as a rubbish tip. Now, on the layer of earth placed atop the landfill, there is scrubby, horse-grazed grassland with dense thickets of briar and thorn, a reasonable diversity of flowers (see Figure 1.1), and several invertebrate-rich ponds within the small depressions of the unnatural topography. Overall, the area could be said to have rebounded into what is a reasonably good site for wildlife.

That is not to say that the place is without flaw. Where a bridge crosses a stream that bisects the site, for instance, the combined erosion from horses, walkers, mountain bikers, and illegal motorized vehicles has brought plastic bottles and other buried household waste back up to the surface—or, rather, brought the surface back down to the rubbish. This presents a stark visual reminder that our problems cannot be buried forever.

Other than this minor working of the earth, though, I had deemed incursions into the land to be unlikely. The gravel had been taken. The landfill potential had been seized. And I dismissed the rumours of a proposed housing development as being simply ludicrous, given what now lies beneath the surface. It might not be dug up again for a thousand years, I reasoned, and only then if there exist such things as archaeologists in future civilizations. All told, there *seemed* to be no solastalgic hazard.

Then, recently, a story appeared in a local paper about how the government was seeking to convert the site into a giant solar farm.

Figure 1.1: A bee orchid, an edgeland emblem, growing from the earth layer of an old landfill site. A quintessential plant of former quarries, this species also has a habit of popping up on mowed road verges. It is said that it can take up to eight years of development before a flower-spike is sent up. Mowing helps the bee orchid outcompete other plants, although if the flower-spike itself is cut before seed is set, all the effort was ultimately pointless. This, for the orchid, is a case of one mow too many.

While this idea can in some ways be seen as a positive development towards greener ways of living, it will certainly be bad news for the wildlife who inhabit or visit the place. This is the reality of the world in which we live. Even the greening of society comes with ecological costs.

From the examples just presented and the preceding discussion of psychoterratic states, one might conclude that it would be prudent to avoid knowing too much and caring too intimately about the world around them. Yet, earlier I suggested that once you begin to sense a solidarity with the wider community of life—or Earthlingness—the blossoming of concern and care is inevitable unless you shut yourself away from non-human nature. And this, as I have already said, is not something that I advocate.

Instead, I am going to propose that we just have to brave the 'storm of now' as best we can. For people with a deep green sensibility, the emotions that arise from living within the more-than-human world are amplified, the bitter ones and sweet ones alike. And when the bitter ones dominate, as they so often do in these times, we have to do what we can to face up to them.

That's easier said than done, you may be thinking. *Weren't you just telling me about a thing called 'eco-paralysis'?*

Well, I do not deny that there are days when I struggle to bring myself to do anything to help my fellow Earthlings and all I want to do is reach for the dairy-free ice cream. I suspect that I am not alone in that. Mercifully, for me, such days are relatively infrequent, which is something that I attribute to the powerful motivation to fight for ecological justice that arises from a deep green psyche. Within the homogenization and draining of life's essence by industrialized human societies—to recall a phrase that I used earlier—an Earth ethic throws into relief the injustices suffered by non-human parties, all of whom are without guilt and silent. And nothing makes my hackles rise quite like innocent, voiceless victims.

I must admit that there are also days when I contemplate the other end of the scale of activity. This I call 'going full Treadwell', after a man with that name for whom I have much sympathy. He was the person who, for more than a decade, spent his summers living with grizzly bears in Alaska, out of a desire to be with them in order to protect them. For any readers who do not know his tale and who are thinking about looking it up, I will not spoil the ending, but I will just say that if the thought of human clothes being recovered from a bear's stomach is something that you find gruesome, then it might not be the right story for you.

Most days, happily, my rudder lies between the extremes. Even though the growth-fuelled furnace of the sixth mass extinction, the ultimate despair machine, is blazing out of control—and even though it seems almost certain that vast and wondrously intricate biological systems will collapse—I see ecological justice as a cause that is still very much worth our attention and efforts. While the current radiation of life (of which humans are so fortunate to be a part) will almost certainly be forced through a tight bottleneck, there are some individuals, some populations, and some species that will make it through. Our actions today can widen that bottleneck. And that is a goal worth scrapping for till our last breaths.

In steering a relatively steady course, I have also drawn benefit from a number of coping mechanisms. These include small practical actions, such as taking litter-picking gear out with me on my walks and submitting sightings of the wildlife that I see for entry into conservation databases. Such actions help me feel like my presence in a wild space is beneficial rather than detrimental. That is important to me on account of a recurring mental malady in which I feel an aversion to visiting a place—and it could be somewhere I love or somewhere that is new to me—because of a fear of causing the place harm by, say, crushing a plant. This disinclination is not something that Albrecht's typology yet covers, although it is closely related to his concept of 'topoaversion', which describes a reluctance to revisit a cherished place that one knows to have undergone negative change at the hands of others. Of course, if I was a student of Jainism, I would not interpret my own disinclination as a negative emotion but instead cherish it within the religion's concept of *ahimsa*—an avoidance of harm to other life forms. And there is a lot that could be said in favour of this framing.

Other coping mechanisms that I employ, beyond practical actions, include mental devices. A preferred one involves me endeavouring to experience the world as a non-human would. Some items of litter, I might reason, are relatively inert and unlikely to trap or harm an animal. Only humans seem to be particularly troubled by aesthetic blemishes, the reasoning continues, and so if I can think like, let's say, a fox, then I can temporarily overlook those items of litter. (This is a handy trick when my rubbish sacks are full.) In a related device, I find myself able to ignore a horizon blighted by industrial development by adjusting my scale of concern to that of some of the smaller life forms that I love, such as colony-based butterflies (see Figure 1.2).

I have written on this in the magazine *Country-Side*, noting the following:

> In wilder areas, away from Britain, I've been able to raise my head to the horizon without fear of witnessing the devastation of development. Around my home, though, I've come to realize that it is much better, from a mental health perspective, to shift my focus to a smaller scale. And so, now, I happily spend summer days in a single small meadow or wood, walking short distances between wild flowers, shrubs, and trees, and observing the richness of invertebrate life, without having to worry about what is happening outside. On these days, the insects and I share a universe.

Figure 1.2: A ringlet butterfly in a nature reserve near the author's home.

Sometime after writing the above passage, I came across an observation that Henry Thoreau made on entomology, which has a certain parallel with my own sentiment:

> Entomology extends the limits of being in a new direction, so that I walk in nature with a sense of greater space and freedom. It suggests besides, that the universe is not rough-hewn, but perfect in its details. Nature will bear the closest inspection; she invites us to lay our eye level with the smallest leaf, and take an insect view of its plain.

There is a final factor that has been important in keeping my rudder steady through the storm of now. That is the support that I have derived from the insights of ecologically minded friends on the question of why we should continue to fight, even if the outlook is so bleak. For, in contrast to Aldo Leopold, whom I quoted above for his ecological education seeing him live "alone in a world of wounds," I do not feel nearly so isolated. Rather, I am fortunate to be in contact with many other people who understand what an Earth ethic signifies (thanks to, among other things, Leopold's writings).

One such friend is Eileen Crist, who is an ecological writer of extraordinary talent. What I believe is her most cogent offering on the topic of eco-activism in the face of slim odds comes from a *CBC News* story by Nicole Mortillaro. In this she was quoted as saying something that I think is very hard to argue with (and very tempting to plagiarize):

> When you take care of your family, you don't do it because you're optimistic or pessimistic… it's because that's what you do. Our mandate is that we take care of Earth and Earthlings and human beings because we're all family.

Another friend is Patrick Curry, who is a distinguished ecological philosopher. He owns what are probably the most daunting personal bookshelves that I have ever encountered and, unsurprisingly, is exceptionally well-read across philosophy. Despite having such material at his fingertips, Patrick finds his own retort to the potential paralysis of despair not in some great metaphysical tome but instead in a novel. That novel is *The Lord of the Rings* and the page that he turns to for counsel is the one on which the following musing of Gandalf appears: "Despair is for those who see the future beyond any doubt. We do not."

I will stop now, because I know that name-dropping can be a little nauseating, although I do hope that you will see how it was necessary in order for me to make the point that I did about Aldo Leopold's own observation. (In case you were wondering: No, Aldo is not another pal. I was born a couple of generations too late for that. But I would have very much liked it if he could have been.)

In this introductory chapter, I have offered no grand cures for negative psychoterratic phenomena such as solastalgia. The reality, I suspect—at least for those going down the deep green path—is that none exists. Furthermore, I have argued against the prophylactic measure of sealing oneself away in human infrastructure so as to avoid growing too strong an emotional bond with the more-than-human world.

So why discuss it at all? The reason I have done so, before I invite you into my back garden, is two-fold. Firstly, I wanted to at least acknowledge that there are some pretty heavy emotions at play here, even if I cannot offer effective psychological counsel. Secondly, I wanted to remind you that, as fierce as is the storm of now, you are not alone. For if you have a deep care for the world around you, not only will you find many like-minded humans but you will also be part of a much larger family of Earthlings.

Fortunately, Earthlingness also offers a potent and omnipresent psychoterratic upside. Eutierria, to recall an example noted above, is the positive feeling of oneness and connectedness that arises from a breaking-down of boundaries between oneself and the more-than-human world. There are simpler emotions too, including the feeling of joy and the appreciation of beauty. As I will endeavour to show in the pages of this book, the potential for experiencing pleasure is without limits, and the well of previously unknown beauty essentially bottomless. For—when free from modern life's clouding distractions, and released from its obstinate grasp—one can tune into nature's wavelength and experience her every breath, from the bobbing flight of a wagtail to the thundering cascade of a waterfall, as a new thrill. In these timeless moments, as one receives pulse after exhilarating pulse from the ecospheric orchestra, philosophy becomes redundant, just as life's meaning is made abundantly clear.

I will give the last word here to Ian Whyte—a good friend, to me and the Earth—and paraphrase a comment from a pertinent note that he sent me: In this most destructive era, a great solace lies in loving the fellow Earthlings who are with us and in wholeheartedly opening ourselves up to their being. ●

Chapter 2:
A brief history
of the land

In a region absolutely covered with trees, human life could not long be sustained...

George Perkins Marsh, from his 1864 book *Man and Nature*

Fundamental to an appreciation of a place—be it a vast forest or a tiny back garden—is an understanding of its history. And, thus, in a self-assessment quiz for testing an individual's bioregional knowledge that was developed by Leonard Charles and colleagues in the early 1980s, no fewer than five of the twenty questions concerned the social, biological, or geological past, as opposed to the present. The current chapter comprises answers to two of these questions. Taken in combination, the responses will describe the landscape context in which my back garden is sited. (I will be cheating somewhat in the endeavour, as I will be responding under open-book conditions, with John Catt's *Hertfordshire Geology and Landscape* proving particularly useful.)

The first question that I will attempt to answer is: *What primary ecological event or process influenced the land form where you live?* I interpret the word 'ecological' in this question to be angling at geological events and processes specifically. If you are not particularly strong on geology, you do not need to worry, as neither am I, and so I will need to be brief in order to avoid showing my hand. What I can tell you is that one major process was the laying down of calcium carbonate from the shells of marine organisms approximately 85–95 million years ago, when the land was covered by a warm, shallow sea. As a result of this, my back garden stands on chalk bedrock. On top of this bedrock, there is a superficial deposit of sand and gravel. This material is part of what is known as the Kesgrave Sands and Gravels, which comprise sediments from the proto-Thames—a large precursor to the modern Thames that cut a varying course to the north of its current path. The sediment—in other words, the river bed—is thought to have been laid down from around the start of the Pleistocene epoch, 1.8 million years ago, up to approximately 450 thousand years ago. At this point, a vast sheet of frozen water is believed to have reached modern-day St Albans, creating a large ice-dammed lake that, through a catastrophic overspill, rerouted the Thames towards its modern course. It is the sole time in Britain's geological history that an ice sheet is thought to have reached these southern climes. In short, then, my back garden sits atop an ancient river bed, which in turn stands on the bottom of a primeval sea.

The second question from the bioregional self-assessment that I will look at is: *What is the land use history of where you live?* The rest of this chapter will be spent attempting to answer this.

I will begin at the start of the Holocene, the present geological epoch, which commenced just shy of twelve thousand years ago, after the retreat of the glaciers of the last ice age. *Homo sapiens* would have been using the land around modern St Albans in the tail-end of the previous epoch, the Pleistocene, applying a largely nomadic approach to seasonal hunting and gathering; but their presence would have been periodic only and they would have occurred at a very low population density.

The last ice age had converted Britain to tundra and, as the landscape historian Oliver Rackham mused, "probably left not a single tree alive." And, thus, the start of the Holocene is also the beginning of the history of Britain's most recent wildwood. Of the more significant woodland trees, the first species to return were Scots pine and birches, which are tolerant of arctic conditions and can disperse readily. Next in the sequence, according to Rackham, was hazel; and then there followed a suite of deciduous species—oaks, alder, small-leaved lime, elms, ash, and others—and an evergreen—holly. Around seven or eight thousand years ago (four or five millennia into the Holocene), huge volumes of water released by the melting of ice sheets flooded a land bridge that had linked Britain to continental Europe, thus cutting it off from the mainland. Tree species that arrived after this point are considered non-native.

The wildwood was dynamic and never uniform, either at a local or a regional scale. Rackham defined various wildwood 'provinces' to describe the region-level variation at around six thousand years ago. My back garden, like much of lowland England, sits in Rackham's 'lime province', where lime was much more common than it is today and often the commonest woodland tree. At this time, the wildwood would have been home to many species that have since died off from the island, predominantly at the hand of humans, as George Monbiot discussed in his book *Feral*. These include wolves, lynx, brown bears, moose, and wild oxen (or aurochs). It is quite possible that representatives of all of these species have at some point ambled or charged across the land where my back garden now stands. Other species that were extirpated, but have since been reintroduced into the wild, are beavers and wild boar. (The last observations might score me points on another of the questions about the past in the bioregional self-assessment exercise: *What species have become extinct in your area?*)

The wildwood took shape during what, for local human cultures, was the Mesolithic, the last Stone Age period before the introduction of arable and pastoral agriculture. Typical artefacts of a North European Mesolithic culture known as the Maglemosian, including flint blades and axe heads, have been found at several sites within a few miles' radius of where I live. As described in Catt's *Hertfordshire Geology and Landscape*, these people may have occupied semi-permanent camps within the wildwood besides lakes or rivers, where they would have been able to catch fish, to hunt waterfowl and mammals, to forage for foods such as hazelnuts, and to obtain a mixture of building materials, including timber and reeds. Historical geographer Michael Williams speculated, in his book *Deforesting the Earth*, that Britain's Mesolithic humans would also have attempted to create small openings in the forest canopy so as to encourage greater productivity in the herb layer and thus entice deer and wild boar, whom they hunted. (The above paragraph might gain points on yet another of the self-assessment questions: *What were the primary subsistence techniques of the culture that lived in your area before you?*)

The extent to which Mesolithic humans shaped Britain's woodland is something that we will perhaps never know, but what we can say for sure is that there were other forces at work that helped create openings in the canopy. These would have included storms, of course, but also, in a potentially much more significant way, the activity of herbivores, not least the now-extinct wild ox. Again, though, there is uncertainty as to the extent of the impact that this force—grazing by beasts—would have had on the make-up of Britain's pre-agricultural land cover.

Highlighting this uncertainty, Rackham described a pair of competing models: the first of these is wildwood as dense forest, following the work of the pioneering ecologist Arthur Tansley; the second is wildwood as savannah, after the more recent work of Frans Vera. Vera's hypothesis, described in his landmark book *Grazing Ecology and Forest History*, was summarized by Rackham as follows: "The wildwood was not all trees, but contained large areas of grassland, maintained by the grazing of wild beasts."

There are various competing strands of evidence supporting one model or the other, and a consensus has not yet emerged on the true nature of Britain's wildwood (perhaps it never will). Even if the evidence is restricted to that of a single kind, such as the record of surviving pollen grains in Mesolithic wildwood samples, the findings point in different directions. In this case, the limited extent of grass pollen, coupled with the abundance of the pollen of elm, a tree that is very sensitive to herbivory, substantiates Tansley's dense-forest hypothesis. The existence of pollen from shade-intolerant herbs, in contrast, is supportive of the Vera model.

Overall, based on my own reading of the evidence (which I completed during an abandoned PhD attempt, for whatever that's worth), I believe that there may well have been large open areas, as well as many small apertures in the canopy, but I think that the overall nature of the wildwood in Britain was closer to Tansley's idea than it was to savannah. Accordingly, I believe that, during most snapshots in time after the postglacial return of trees and before agricultural clearance (I say *most* because the wildwood was dynamic), the land where my back garden is sited would have been under a dense canopy.

If the Tansley model does provide a more accurate picture of what Britain's wildwood looked like, then the task of creating clearings that was faced by the early agriculturalists of the Neolithic period, around six thousand years ago, would have been an extremely labour-intensive one. (One might reasonably wonder, then, why these people went to the trouble, given the abundance of food available through hunting and gathering. This is a good question.) If, on the other hand, it is Vera's model that has a stronger applicability to Britain's wildwood, then these early agriculturalists would have benefitted from a wealth of open virgin land for the cultivation of crops and pastoral farming. Regardless of how the openings arose, though, it can be said that the crops that would have been grown on the land in the vicinity of my back garden, as the Holocene unfolded, probably comprised some mixture of oats, rye, bread wheat, and legumes.

The next point on our journey to the present comes around two thousand years ago. Whatever the nature of the pre-agricultural wildwood had been, it seems that the land area that is modern England had, by this point, seen its level of forest cover reduced to somewhere around the ten or fifteen per cent mark. Moreover, the large majority of the surviving woodlands, according to Rackham, were no longer 'wild' but, rather, were under a management regime that he labelled woodmanship. This regime, I should note, is wholly different from modern industrial forestry, as it involves working with the species naturally present, and it favours regrowth of established trees through practices such as coppicing.

If I had a time machine with which to visit managed woodland near the site of my back garden one spring two thousand years ago, I can speculate that the ground flora I would encounter might include wood anemone (see Figure 2.1), yellow archangel, and bluebell—the last of these being a particular icon of British forest—as well as a delightful and delicate grass known as wood melick. This I can state because such plants hang on today in remnant fragments of ancient woodland around my home, and all are widely distributed across modern Britain, indicating that their local presence does not rely on some current climatic peculiarity.

On this same time-travel trip, if I walked from those woods over to a hill that I know just to the south-west of the modern site of St Albans, I would find there the fortified settlement of Verlamion. This was a power centre for the Catuvellauni, a Celtic tribe, and large earthworks in the surrounding area today are among the marks on the land thought to have been left by them. One such earthwork—a mile-long ditch that is ten metres deep in places and that was quite

Figure 2.1: Wood anemone, an ancient woodland flower that grows in the vicinity of the author's back garden.

plausibly part of a Celtic defensive system—is known as Beech Bottom and is a short stroll from my home.

The Catuvellauni stronghold of Verlamion succumbed to the invasion of Britain by the Romans, who, in turn, established a settlement called Verulamium on nearby land. This place grew to become one of the largest urban centres in Roman Britain, despite the early setback of being razed during an uprising of the Iceni, another Celtic tribe, led by Queen Boudicca.

After the eventual withdrawal of the Romans from Britain, an Anglo-Saxon tribe known as the Waeclingas occupied the site of the future settlement of St Albans, which itself began to take shape in the Middle Ages. Maps that have survived from the centuries that followed the end of the Middle Ages reveal the area around St Albans to be largely devoid of woodland. This is perhaps unsurprising, in light of the busy history of human occupancy.

For the next point in the story we jump to the closing years of the nineteenth century. The land where my back garden sits was then, according to an account by local historian Mike Neighbour, part of a plot called Marston Nine Acre Field. Probably arable in nature, the field was jointly owned by St Albans Grammar School and the Earl of Verulam. It was bordered on the south by an old turnpike road, and on the opposite side of this road there was another school-owned field, which is believed to have been used, at that point in time, for grazing by cows. That field was acquired by Smith's Printing Agency for construction of the Fleet Printing Works, which was named after the Fleet Street location of the company's London site. The firm was presumably attracted to the plot by the existence of a single-track railway immediately to the south that was used both for passenger transport and for moving goods.

I mention the print works for two reasons. The first is that my own home sits in a row of terraced houses that was built as accommodation for employees at the works. I should note here that the back garden of my home, if it was like the typical garden of an artisan's house at that time, might have been used for growing a mixture of fruit and vegetables, as well as some ornamental flowering plants. The second reason I mention the print industry connection is that the urban area that grew up around it was named Fleetville, after the name of the works (which thus, in turn, acknowledges Fleet Street). In the years that followed, further houses were built on the land between Fleetville and St Albans, and the former soon became just a suburb of the latter.

Whew! Ninety-five million years in a little over two thousand words. And now that we have gone through the history of the land together, I am finally ready to invite you into my back garden. ●

Chapter 3:
A wild pocket
of suburbia

Odd as I am sure it will appear to some, I can think of no better form of personal involvement in the cure of the environment than that of gardening.

Wendell Berry, from his 1969 essay 'Think Little'

"Can you get me a few sprigs of rosemary?" my wife asks. Later, we will be roasting some commercially grown potatoes with shop-bought garlic, and it will feel good to be able to add a soupçon of self-sufficiency to the tray.

I grab a pair of scissors from a clay pot that holds our kitchen implements and head out into the restorative warmth of a spring afternoon. Staying on task, I stroll to the far end of the back garden, where there grows a rosemary bush which pre-dates our own presence in this place. At the bush, however, something distracts me: there is a hint of movement in the friable soil below. After a few moments' study, my eyes settle on a small opening, the size of a chickpea. It looks like an entrance into a burrow, and descending into it is the hairy rear of some insect or other. I snip a few sprigs of the Mediterranean shrub—giver of one of the planet's most gorgeous aromas, as judged by my human nostrils. As I pivot to head back to the kitchen I notice a strikingly glossy, elegantly winged, yellow-and-black insect perched on the tip of an upper shoot of the rosemary.

A few further observations, coupled with some simple desk research that I conduct while digesting the potatoes, help me identify the architect of the hole, and I am able to piece the full story together. The hairy rear was that of a female *Andrena* mining bee, who had excavated the burrow and was making one of numerous visits to stock the lateral tunnels inside with pollen and nectar that she had foraged from nearby flowers. *Andrena* bees, on completing the stocking of a tunnel, lay a fertilized egg, which they seal off with the food within a nest cell. In this way, the offspring gain a protected environment for their formative nourishment.

So far, so good. But what about the glossy, yellow-and-black insect on the shrub above? It turns out that she was a cuckoo bee of the *Nomada* genus. It was very likely that she had been attracted to the burrow by some olfactory cue. To her, the *Andrena* bee's chemical signature is probably more gorgeous than the smell of crushed rosemary is to me. The reason that this olfactory cue is of such interest to the *Nomada* bee relates to the fact that she does not herself collect pollen for her offspring. Instead, she lays eggs in the nest cells made by *Andrena* bees. *Nomada* larvae, on hatching, kill the *Andrena* egg and secure exclusive access to the free larder. Thus, the offspring of the female *Nomada* gain, at the expense of another bee, a protected environment for their formative nourishment. This type of food theft is called 'kleptoparasitism', and there is a nice paper on the *Nomada–Andrena* example that was written by Jan Tengö and Gunnar Bergström in *Science* in the 1970s.

I present the story above as just one example of goings-on among the cohabiters of my back garden in St Albans. The garden, as I have already noted, measures thirteen paces by four. Thirteen paces is the distance from the French windows of the kitchen, going in a westerly direction, to the rear fence. The narrow rectangle that is described by this length and the orthogonal dimension of four paces constitutes the first, and so far only, piece of open land that my wife and I have 'owned' (to put a human term on the relationship). Since the other end of our house opens directly onto a pavement, we have no front garden.

To put it another way, the garden that I am writing about makes up a mere tenth of a trillionth of the Earth's surface area. If you would like an aid to understanding this number that uses the leguminous measuring scale that I introduced above (with the chickpea-sized entrance to the bee burrow), then I can say that if one was to line up pinto beans, end to end, between the Earth and the Sun, an individual bean in this gargantuan column would be one tenth of a trillionth of the total length. Or, if the best way to understand land areas is by making reference to Belgium, as so many journalists would have us believe, then my garden is to the Earth's surface what the bottom of a pint glass is to that country of great beer.

All of this I can calculate with precision because my natural stride, when I am in measuring mode, is a perfect metre. I would not describe anything else about my body as being perfect, or even close to it, but in a quirk of fate I also have a conveniently sized thumb, as far as measuring is concerned. This I learned during an exercise I completed for my Forestry master's degree as part of a module on forest mensuration—a topic into which I will now make a brief foray.

One of the things that foresters like to know about stands of trees is the basal area per acre. This is a measure of density based on the cross-sectional area of trees at 1.3 metres above the ground, which is known as 'breast height'. If you can imagine someone with a chainsaw cutting down all the trees in an acre of woodland at breast height (an acre, it would be remiss of me to neglect to mention, is equivalent to a little over one ten-millionth of Belgium), then the sum of the surface areas of all the resulting stump-tops would give you the total basal area for that acre. Fortunately, it is possible to make a pretty good estimate of basal area per acre without firing up a chainsaw. You can use, instead, something called an angle gauge, which is a small flat piece of metal that has a window cut out of it and a lightweight chain attached. Standing in the woodland that you want to measure, you put the loose tip of the chain in your mouth and hold the gauge straight out in front of you with the chain taut, which ensures that it remains a certain distance from your eye. Next, keeping your feet on the same spot, you slowly start to turn in a circle, counting all those trees, and only those trees, that are so big that they appear wider than the window of the gauge. Once you have turned a full circle, you multiply the number of trees that you counted by a basal area factor, which is supplied with the gauge, in order to get your basal area per hectare. It is a remarkable measuring trick that involves some rather elegant mathematics.

On the Forestry course, we were asked, in order for us to test our understanding of the principles involved, to calculate the multiplier—the basal area factor—for our own thumb when held upward with arm extended horizontally. The basal area factors for commercial gauges are always nice round numbers, like five, but for a thumb it could, of course, be anything. I took great care in calculating a value that was accurate and that had two decimal points of precision, and I was delighted to find that it came out as a perfect round number. Only one student in a hundred will have such a privilege, and, in honour of the discovery, a coursemate and I christened my digit a 'forester's thumb'.

I will return, now, to the back garden to provide a few more metrics, and for these I will resist the temptation of tangents so as to be able to rattle through them. First, the garden sits only about a hundred metres (330 feet) above sea level. Secondly, it receives around 70 centimetres (28 inches) of rain a year, which means that it is relatively dry for a place in Britain. Thirdly, it has an average daily maximum temperature of 22°C (72°F) in July, the warmest month, and an average daily minimum of 1°C (34°F) in February, the coldest month, which exemplifies the relatively cool summers and mild winters of Britain's oceanic climate.

I could also provide precise geographical coordinates so that you could look it up on a map. If you were paying attention in the previous chapter, you will know that my home is in a suburb of St Albans called Fleetville and was built to house employees of a printing works. Aping Ed Abbey's reluctance to give full details of his own special places, though, I will be no more explicit than that. What I will say, because it is relevant to its local ecology, is that the garden is embedded in a two-by-twenty-five grid of similarly sized plots, with its own place within the matrix demarcated by tall wooden fencing. The surrounding area is of a decidedly urban character and so the garden does not benefit from frequent incidental visits of wildlife from a nearby wood, say, or a meadow. In other words, it works hard for the wildlife that it supports.

Completing the statistics, I will recall the remark in Chapter 2 about the house and garden being built at the very end of the nineteenth century and add that my wife and I have lived there for the past thirteen years.

Caring for a small garden to benefit wildlife is a bit like voting in a democracy. Each individual plot does not count for much in the grand scheme, much like each individual vote is by itself almost worthless. Yet if enough people vote in a democracy, the sum effect of a multitude of almost-worthless actions can be to keep the worst kinds of politics at bay. Likewise, if enough people do their bit for wildlife on their own patch of land, then the combined impact is potentially one of huge benefit for nature.

This point about the potential for gardens *en masse* was made to me during a conversation with a fellow nature-lover some years ago, at a time when my interest in gardening for wildlife was beginning to blossom. Our discussion took place over beer on a warm summer evening in a garden in Norfolk. What he said was… Well, I cannot remember what words he used exactly, but the message about gardens having an important role in the bigger picture of conservation stayed with me as tenaciously as tinnitus. In addition to this point, our conversation ran through all the standard motifs of a meeting between naturalists. We discussed new books: there was, for instance, an identification guide to hoverflies that had just been published. We moaned about society and the government. And he, being the local, gave me helpful suggestions, in great detail and at length, on the best nature reserves to visit in the area. The only problem with all of this was that the garden we were in was the location for the reception of a wedding. I had a fairly tenuous connection to the married couple, but he was the bride's father and had totally neglected his duty to circulate among the more significant guests. This is the type of thing that happens when nature-lovers come together.

If you prefer cold statistics to sketchy beer-fuelled anecdotes, then you may be interested in the findings from a study by Zoe Davies and colleagues published in 2009 that combined the results from various surveys on the nature of British gardens. The authors estimated— based on a calculated average garden size well over three times the size of my own—that residential gardens comprised more than 4300 square kilometres of the country's land. This is an area about the same as that of Britain's largest national park, the Cairngorms. They further determined that the combined habitat of all the gardens was home to nearly a quarter of Britain's non-woodland trees and also contained approximately three million ponds, with these having an average size of one square metre. The relative importance of gardens in conservation, they rightly reasoned, will only grow with the rush to build ever more houses in the present era.

In relatively affluent human settlements, I think that there should be a special obligation to care for residential gardens in as ecologically beneficial a fashion as possible. I say this for the reason that higher affluence is linked to a larger ecological footprint. I also mention it because the city where I live is such a settlement. A report written for WWF-UK in 2007, by Alan Calcott and Jamie Bull, calculated that St Albans had the second largest *per capita* footprint of any British city (being 'bested' only by Winchester). One of the domains that St Albans fared especially badly in was transport. Sadly, despite the existence of a variety of public transport options, the level of ownership of private vehicles is very high. And many gardens have been destroyed in recent decades to create extra space for parking these (often over-sized) vehicles.

But you can only control what you can control—says the person intent on defying eco-paralysis—and my wife and I like to direct much of our attention to lowering our own portion of the city's ecological footprint and to caring for our back garden in a way that supports wildlife. Much of what we do inside and outside our home is non-conformist and could be considered 'experimental living'. Such "individual experiments in living," according to political scholar Luke Plotica, "furnish both evidence of a particular way of living and, more importantly, evidence that still other ways are possible." Some of the more experimental facets of our life are presented in these pages; others I might perhaps describe at a later time. Crucially, we are not relying on local or national governments to be a source of salvation, *in themselves*, just as we are not looking to buy our way out of the ecological predicament. Relatedly, Plotica—a spirited defender of individual action as a necessary adjunct to institutional politics (and thus a person after my own heart)—has written:

> Making apple cider vinegar at home will not save the ecosphere, but the tacit belief that the only possible modes of ecological citizenship come pre-packaged in political platforms and retail product lines will surely destroy it.

The result of the endeavours of my wife and myself, in relation to the garden, is a backyard that packs a lot into a small space. Woody plant life includes, in addition to the rosemary bush mentioned earlier, a shrubby hedge, a mature cherry tree, several climbers, and an assortment of saplings. The herb layer, which grows in numerous pots and beds containing soils of varying levels of sandiness, comprises a seasonal succession of diverse plants that feed us and other animals. There is also a thriving wildlife pond, and I can say that its addition to the garden's make-up has undoubtedly been the most important of all the changes that we have made. As well as supporting the life cycles of a range of amphibians (see Figure 3.1), insects, and other invertebrates, the pond doubles up as a drinking hole for various animals and as a bathing spot for birds. Additionally, there are numerous hidey-holes in the garden for small animals; there are various piles of fallen leaves, which are used by insects and other life forms to shelter themselves from the hazards of winter; there are stacks of dead wood, which provide nourishment for fungi, beetle larvae, and other organisms; and there is a bird feeder, which has

Figure 3.1: A common frog with its head partially
above the surface of the garden pond.

been hung in a spot that we consider to be the most inaccessible
for visiting domestic cats (it is cleaned regularly so as to avoid it
becoming a wellspring of disease). The garden also contains several
'infrastructural' elements. There are paved areas for us to walk, and
put chairs, on. We have a composting zone. There is also a small
shed, the roof of which serves as the collection area for our rainwater-
capturing system (only I find it funny to call this wooden structure
the 'watershed'). And we have a small nursery area for seedlings.
Last of all, the garden is home to two small flower-pot men.

All of this, with the exception of the flower-pot men, has been guided
by five principles of care. We did not start out with these principles.
They reflect, instead, a philosophy that has evolved during our first
thirteen years. It is also a philosophy that has developed from an
increasingly strong desire, in accord with the deep green worldview, to
act principally in the interests of the non-human cohabiters and visitors.

The first principle of care, which is a two-parter, has been *to not
change things too quickly and to carefully observe the impact of our actions*.
The essence of this principle is echoed by biologist Dave Goulson in
his recent book *The Garden Jungle*, which has the ambitiously stated

subtitle of 'Gardening to save the planet'. In this book, Goulson describes how his own approach to gardening for wildlife, wherever he has lived, has always been "to gently steer the garden to support the most wildlife possible, learning as [he] went." The principle also reflects, to some extent, one of Aldo Leopold's better-known phrases: "To keep every cog and wheel is the first precaution of intelligent tinkering." This is often cited in regard to the need to safeguard endangered species, but I feel that it also has applicability in urging caution about removing 'undesirable' plants from a garden. One of the potential issues with such removals is that the plants might be the only source of sustenance for a particular insect in the local area.

Our second principle of care has been *to garden with a light hand*, which is another guiding notion that is shared by Goulson. As he notes in *The Garden Jungle*: "Successful wildlife gardening is as much about what you don't do as what you do." In our garden, avoiding the use of toxic substances and chemical fertilizer has been a crucial factor in the development of a wildlife haven. We also engage in only minimal turning of the soil. In addition, we have not responded aggressively to self-sown gifts, but rather have mostly embraced these 'weeds' (as most people call them). In this way, the garden could be considered as being fairly wild, at least as far as urban habitat goes.

I have sometimes wondered if any self-sown surprises have grown from seeds laid down during a time before the house was built. In some spots where we have dug into the soil—such as under paving stones—we have encountered a sheet of thick plastic six inches below the surface. The plastic was presumably installed during previous works to the garden, and its presence suggests that the earth that is exposed above it in such places has been added, and that this soil's nature may thus bear no connection to the underlying geology of old riverbed and primeval sea bottom. In other subsurface explorations, though, it has seemed that we were digging into ancient humus. If this is the case, the earth here represents a link to the land's agricultural past. Thus, it is not impossible that a plant or two that grows in the garden is some relict that has clung on in the seed bank from the land's pre-garden life. Perhaps one of the many groundsels that have sprung up, for example, have done so after remaining a dormant possibility, in the form of a seed, for more than a century.

Returning to the principles, the third one has been *to keep as much of the dead and living biomass on site as possible*. This practice is reflected in the creation of the aforementioned leaf piles. We have also, for instance, placed branches pruned from the hedge into the pond, which has created aquatic perches for birds and damselflies to use and offered a foothold for marginal vegetation. And then there are the stems of bamboo that have sprung up as escapees from a clump in a neighbour's garden. These are cut and used to make struts for the support of climbers, as well as structures for growing vegetables. As a final example, by making a raised bed we were able to find room for the earth that was removed in digging up the pond so that it remained in the garden.

This third principle, I should note, does not exclude the addition of leaves or other material from outside of the garden. An especially valuable addition in our own case has been dead wood, and a potential source for this is native trees growing on nearby streets. While councils would seem to have a tendency to prune such trees as if their tools will stop working if not constantly in use, a large branch is occasionally left on a tree long enough for it to be brought to the ground by gravity. To maximize your chance of finding one, it is well worth patrolling the streets as morning breaks after a big storm. The early hours are also a good time for discreetly obtaining bricks, and other useful materials for wildlife gardens, directly out of skips. (For non-British readers who are unfamiliar with the term 'skip', it is a large transportable container that can be hired for dumping waste material, and it is typically served as a side dish when people order a renovation of their house). A friend asked me why I do not just go along in the middle of the day and ask permission from the household that hired the skip. Answer: It would not nearly be as much fun.

The fourth principle has been *to favour plants that are native, especially those that lack a great thirst*, whenever the opportunity has arisen for us to introduce new herbaceous life. But while the championing of native plants has become a maxim of wildlife gardening, we have found that it can still be a challenge to achieve. A typical garden centre, for instance, offers limited information, and a sparse choice, when it comes to such plants. In our own case, we have sometimes settled for non-native species, as long as they meet three criteria. First, they should be non-invasive, which means that they are not going to escape and multiply rampantly in another habitat. Secondly, they should be known to have a particular benefit for wildlife, such as by offering nectar earlier or later than typical native plants do. And, thirdly, they should ideally be naturalized, which means that, while non-native, they have already become established in the region.

The fifth and final principle has been *to be prepared to defend the garden from threats*. The most obvious regular threat comes from visiting felines, who take a great interest in the amphibians, birds, and occasional mammals. To paraphrase Lord Byron, we love not cats the less, but wildlife more, and our defensive strategies include intermittent dusk vigils to oversee the safety of bathing blackbirds and robins. Another of the threats that the garden has faced was an isolated incident but one that was more troubling. The owner of a nearby property was adding a room to their house by building upwards ("land is expensive, but air is cheap," as Wendell Berry mused in his essay 'Two Minds'). One afternoon, as this was going on, I was looking out over the garden when I noticed a rain beginning to fall. But it was not a rain that I knew. Rather than drops of water, it comprised tiny fragments of old insulating material that had been exposed to the outside world by the works. The rain fell, off and on, for days, and much of the garden became covered in a layer of fine debris. I pleaded with the owner and builders to take some measure, such as attaching plastic sheeting to the scaffolding, that would stop the debris falling down into the surrounding gardens, but all I got was either silence or swear words. The local council could not take any action as, technically, no law had been broken. All my wife and I could do was repeatedly sweep the hard surfaces and, once the rain had finished, painstakingly remove the top layer of soil from the garden to try to eliminate as much of the debris as possible. The latter was a challenge for my patience but my wife excelled at it. We still do not know how toxic the debris might have been.

These upward extensions are becoming more common and I believe that in many cases the addition of a room is not really needed and thus is presumably motivated, primarily, by a desire to 'add value' to the property. More generally, homes and gardens seem to be increasingly seen not as a place to live but as a rung on a ladder to greater wealth and improved status. It is my contention that, under such motivations for occupancy, human neighbourhoods and communities do not thrive.

I will close my discussion of the five principles by presenting an example that demonstrates how they can sometimes work in combination. Where we have lifted paving stones and bricks to increase the area of open earth, we have kept the materials on site and used them to augment the garden's offering of hidey-holes. The stones can be placed atop bricks to create a refuge that is particularly suited to frogs and toads who are escaping the threat of marauding kitties.

I would not want you, the reader, to get the impression from the passage above that our actions in the garden have been without flaw. Indeed, I have a number of regrets. To name one, I wish that we had introduced only native plants to the wildlife pond.

Furthermore, I do not wish to imply that the garden is paradisal. It is not. There are many times when I need to listen to music on heavy-duty headphones in order to drown out the screams of argument-prone families and the abrasive, migraine-inducing orchestra of angle grinders and electric saws being used in upward extensions. At other times, especially around the beginning of warmer spells, I might find a moment of sensory enjoyment being broken by a nauseating waft of lighter fluid, harbinger of the odour of barbecue-scorched flesh. When this robs the evening air of honeysuckle's intensifying scent, it is a particular shame—certainly for me, perhaps the moths too.

For all of that, this small back garden in Fleetville, St Albans, is a place from which my wife and I gain food and joy. And much more significantly than that, it is a place where wildlife rules. In this way, it could be described as a home shared by human and non-human Earthling cohabiters, or a garden of greater-than-human import, or, more concisely, a *deep green neighbourhood*. ⬡

Part two

---◇---

Life in the
deep green
neighbourhood

Chapter 4: Biophilia and the Earth ethic

We've strangled all her trees and starved her creatures
There's poison in the sea and the air
But worst of all we've learned to live without her
We've lost the very meaning of our lives

Lyrics from the Kansas song *Death of Mother Nature Suite* (1974)

It is spring in the deep green neighbourhood—a garden of thirteen paces by four. After an early-morning shower, the air slowly warms under a cloudless sky. And life is thriving.

Take the paving stones, as an example. Fused to their surface, lichens expand with unhurried elegance, turning slabs to soil in a primeval succession of infinitesimal increments. Immediately above the stones, cushions of moss salvage the last drips that fall from old guttering and in turn offer springtails a habitat of heavenly moistness. And between the slabs, wild flowers shoot upwards with a banquet that lures an assortment of visitors. Those who feast on nectar—from marmalade hoverflies to hairy-footed flower bees—are welcomed by the plants as vectors of pollen. Those who draw sustenance from the leaves, in contrast, are not. This latter company includes hole-chewing metallic flea beetles, mildew-forming fungi, and minuscule mites of the *Cecidophyes* genus, who induce swellings called galls that serve as sealed nests for their young. But the consumption is not profligate, the flowers mostly stand tall, and the visitors provide meals for other players in life's web. The mildew, for instance, is grazed on by citron-yellow ladybirds with eleven black pupils on each wing case (one of eight species of ladybird that I observed in the garden while writing the book).

Or take, if you would prefer, an untidy corner. A green shieldbug, thinking of the next generation, lays a honeycomb clutch of pale, barrel-shaped eggs on the underside of a leaf (see Figure 4.1). Black ants shuttle morsels of food untiringly back to their nest. An ant damsel bug (see Figure 4.2) is on the hunt, with her thick, straw-like mouth ever-poised for skewering prey. (In all my wanderings around county, country, and continent, I have never known a place to nurture these curious micro-predators as my back garden does.)

Figure 4.1: A clutch of twenty-eight common green shieldbug eggs in the garden. It is believed that the number of eggs laid by this species is typically a multiple of seven.

Figure 4.2: A pre-adult ant damsel bug—a species in a different order (the Hemiptera, or 'true bugs') from ants (the Hymenoptera). The animal gets its name from the pre-adult mimicry of ants, also known as 'myrmecomorphy'. Pale coloration, for instance, gives the impression of a narrow ant-like waist. The effect can help reduce the risk of predation, as certain predators will generally avoid ants.

Zebra spiders bound from plant to rock and back again in search of a meal of their own. And millipedes digest the autumn leaf-fall from the cherry tree. Meanwhile, centipedes await nightfall in the damp refuge of fungus-studded logs, as striped woodlice lie low under loose bricks.

Then there is the pond. A wasp drinks from the surface at one end and a robin bathes at the other. Beneath the water's surface, smooth newts keep their amphibian skin wet. Tadpoles feed hungrily on an alga known as blanket weed, which clings to the edge. And damselfly larvae wolf down a plethora of smaller life forms, including the larvae of a large non-biting midge that is in a genus named *Chironomus*. These larvae are known as bloodworms on account of their scarlet colour, something that relates to the presence of haemoglobins. The haemoglobins, which, as in human blood, have a high affinity for oxygen, help the bloodworm to eke out an existence in the relatively anaerobic mud at the bottom of the pond. This mud forms from varied detritus, including autumn-shed leaves of the cherry tree that land on the pond surface and slowly sink. The haemoglobins make the midge larvae a food item that is high in iron content. And thus does autumn leaf-fall enrich the pond's web of life.

As dusk approaches, a cloud of small flies assembles above the pond, and moths of exquisite variety begin to move from plant to plant in the surrounding vegetation. Soon, pipistrelle bats will spin and turn through the darkening sky to claim their share of the aerial bounty. And, later, yellow-hued slugs and all their nocturnal cousins will emerge, perhaps tempting a hedgehog through a hole in the fence on a quest for nightly rations.

But it could be another way. For there is an alternative in which humans exert ruthless control and enact a regime of sterility. In this starkly contrasting possibility, life is quashed…

Immaculate fencing means that there is no entranceway for hedgehogs. The slugs are poisoned with metaldehyde, a toxic substance whose ban in Britain has been overturned, at least for now, by corporate lawyers. Wasps can be killed, along with other flying insects, by drowning them in a lure—a siren to their olfactory senses. The water in the pond can be continually doctored with chemicals to keep the blanket weed at bay. Or the pond can just be filled in and covered with plastic grass.

In addition, there is no place in this garden for old bricks or logs. And to remove the hassle of having to collect leaves each year, the cherry can be hacked down and its stump poisoned to suppress the tree's desperate attempts at regrowth. Lines of powdered permethrin can be laid down to kill the black ants, taking the zebra spiders with them. The shieldbug eggs can be crushed with a thumb (the 'green way'!) or sprayed with insecticide. Any flowers growing away from sanctioned locations can be killed with glyphosate. The moss can be scraped off the stones. And the lichens can be treated with strong bleach. (If you think that this last approach is far-fetched, note that the Royal Horticultural Society lists bleach, alongside hydrochloric acid, as a suggested substance for the control of lichens, although there is a caveat expressed that its use is not recommended near plants.)

How could different humans react in such radically different ways to garden life? Since the scenario of life is, I believe, further from the typical suburban situation than that of death, I will pose that question in another way: What has motivated the approach that my wife and I have taken in our own garden?

If you paid attention during the introductory chapters, it should come as no surprise that the answer lies partly in our emotional experience of the more-than-human world and partly in a recognizing of the moral standing of non-human nature. I will examine these two factors in turn before exploring the interplay between them. I will then close the chapter with a look at how the emotional bond with non-human others and the consideration of a wider moral universe translate to the human role in gardens.

Before you dive into the rest of the chapter, which covers the most academic ground of any section of this book, I recommend pausing to make yourself a large mug of tea (I will be brewing a lime-flower infusion at this point, but the choice is yours). The discussion below, I should note, is intended mostly for those of a rationalistic bent, who, without it, might find my account of living in nature to be excessively romantic. In regard to my own position on the spectrum from hard-headed rationalism to unfettered sentimentality, I do not mind admitting to a deep uncertainty. Some days, I default to the rationalistic mindset that I developed during a childhood buried in mathematics and computer code, and this is certainly not something of which I am ashamed. Other days—especially those spent in wild and wonderful places—I throw caution to the wind and let myself be guided by involuntary passion.

Emotional experience of the more-than-human world

The term that I will use to describe my emotional experience with respect to the garden is *biophilia*. It appears in the title of the book and was introduced in the Preface as the powerful affinity that humans have with the other-than-human in nature. This affinity can equally be described as a love, and it hardly needs explaining that loving something can translate directly into a desire to see it flourish.

Biophilia, I should add, is one of the positive 'states' that are listed in Glenn Albrecht's psychoterratic typology, which was discussed in Chapter 1. (In truth, 'state' is much too reductive a term to describe something as powerful, rich, and complex as love; but there you go.) For reasons that I explain immediately below, I choose this concept to describe my emotional experience ahead of several other affinities that Albrecht lists.

Two of the discounted affinities are less about life in general, which is my chief concern, and more about a sense of place. One of these is 'topophilia', which is a word popularized by the geographer Yi-Fu Tuan—through a 1974 book named after the concept—as a description of "the affective bond between people and place or setting." The other term is 'endemophilia', which Albrecht himself coined for the affinity with that which is distinctive of one's place.

Another discounted affinity is 'ecophilia'. This is traced by Albrecht back to the work of educational scholar David Sobel, who described it as a "biological tendency to bond with the natural world." With this definition, it seems inseparable from the concept of biophilia. However, Sobel's motivation for using 'eco' rather than 'bio' in the affinity that he described was to contrast it with 'ecophobia', which he defined as "a fear of ecological problems and the natural world" and which he illustrated with ozone depletion. This definition opens the door to an affective realm that goes beyond the biosphere— Earth's interconnected organisms and their habitats—to encompass Earth's life-giving matrix, from its inner core to the outer reaches of its atmosphere, as well as all its life forms and processes, in a grand sum that can be called the 'ecosphere'. If defined in that way, the term ecophilia would describe my own sphere of affective concern well, but since such a usage is not yet widely established, I have favoured biophilia for my present purpose.

A final discounted affinity is 'sumbiophilia', another term coined by Albrecht, which describes a love of living together with other life forms. Since it is a subset of biophilia, I have opted for the mother term, but it does have an important relevance to a relationship with garden life, and I will return to it later in the chapter.

Having explained how biophilia is my preferred descriptor for the affective experience of my back garden, I should next briefly mention its own roots, as I have done for similar terms. Andrew Colman, in the *Oxford Dictionary of Psychology*, notes that the term first gained prominence through its usage by the psychoanalyst Erich Fromm, starting with a magazine article in 1964 in which he defined it as "an orientation which we may call love of life." Two decades later, in a book that was titled simply *Biophilia*, the biologist EO Wilson advanced the idea by explicitly arguing that this affinity had a genetic basis. The conjecture that biophilia is an innate sensibility echoes a diary entry that John Muir made, almost a century earlier, while he was in Alaska in the summer of 1890:

> There is a love of wild Nature in everybody, an ancient mother-love ever showing itself whether recognized or [not], and however covered by cares and duties.

For John Muir, the experience of biophilia peaked during periods of self-immersion in wilderness places, where the presence of the human hand was insignificant. But the affinity manifests itself divergently in different minds. At the other end of the spectrum from Muir are people who are most content spending their time in city parks smelling the nectar of planted flowers and watching birds fly between neatly trimmed bushes. There is no wrong or right way to love nature.

Something shared by Muir types—the set to which I, in truth, belong—and by urban-focused biophiles is a strong desire to spend time experiencing the more-than-human world. Such experiences lead, instinctively and in their own right, to learning more about the life that surrounds us. In addition, though, many nature-lovers opt to enhance and expand their understanding with the aid of educational materials, such as field guides, and by learning from fellow biophiles. This mixture of instinctive and purposeful learning is what makes up the heart of natural history—the human quest to understand the biogeological world around us. It is also what crafts the canvas on which biophilia is painted. Switching metaphors, if I may, biophilia fuels natural history and natural history fuels biophilia.

An important aspect of natural history is learning the names for other life forms and how to tell them apart from similar beings. As I have asserted elsewhere, in a piece that I co-wrote with Ian Whyte, such identities have an important role in helping humans see their fellow

Earth-dwelling organisms as *subjects* and not *objects*. Identities alone, however, do not bestow a full appreciation of the world around us. For that understanding, and thus for a deeper flourishing of biophilia, it is also necessary to study ecological connections. And here, I believe, is where the greatest joys and the richest wonders of naturalism lie.

In the great atom-reorganizing project that is life on Earth, such connections are everywhere. I will start with a simple one from my back garden: a hole that has been chewed in the leaf of a foxglove. The connection is an act of herbivory in which nutritional gains made by the plant have been transferred to a different organism, a mollusc in this case. Here's another: a wiggly brown mine along the edge of a mugwort leaf. Leaf mines are tunnels and galleries made by insect larvae in plant tissue as they feed on their way to maturity. The mine in the mugwort leaf was made by a tiny Agromyzid fly.

Gardeners who cannot find beauty in chewed holes and leaf mines—seeing them, instead, as blemishes only—are probably gardening for themselves rather than for wildlife. To put it another way, if I visit a garden and see nothing other than perfectly formed leaves, I see a garden that is not giving back to the landscape and its denizens. And I grow suspicious that the garden either has been drenched in life-killing chemicals or comprises plants of such an exotic character that they have no endemic herbivores. I should be clear that I am not objecting to empathy with the tree or shrub or herb that has experienced the act of herbivory, but to sanitize nature so that vegetarians cannot feed would be to bring the world down to its knees.

The chewing of holes and mining of leaves are examples of *inter*-species connections, but there are, of course, also *intra*-species connections. In the garden, a striking one in late spring and early summer is the mating of large red damselflies. In order to copulate, the male damselfly secures himself to the female's neck using claspers at the end of his body—the connection here is literal—and the female bends herself round in a circle to bring her reproductive organs to his, forming what naturalists with a romantic disposition sometimes describe as a heart shape (see Figure 4.3). Another mating connection that I encounter most summers, around the solstice, is that between male and female *Helophilus pendulus* hoverflies (see Figure 4.4).

Figure 4.3: A mating pair of large red damselflies in the garden.

Figure 4.4: A mating pair of *Helophilus pendulus* hoverflies. One common name for this species is the footballer, on account of the stripes down the thorax.

Note that the name *Helophilus pendulus* does not mean 'Sun-loving swinger', as I initially thought it did (Classics was not on the curriculum at my school), but actually translates to 'dangling marsh-lover'.

Birdsong is another intra-species connection, whereas bird calls may be of an intra-species or inter-species kind. And then there are the connections between living organisms and non-living entities. One example of this that never ceases to bring me joy is the bathing of birds in the water of the pond. Another is the use of stones for shelter by amphibians.

For nature-lovers, each of these connections is a touchpoint that provides a window into life's wondrous complexity—a complexity that is elegant and harmonious and thus radically different from that encountered in the organization of a human city, say, or in the dynamics of corporate functioning. In my own case, there are few things in the world that give me more joy than watching beetles or bugs that are monophagous—by which I mean those whose diet is restricted to a single food-plant—feeding on that plant, like a key in a lock that opens up a new trophic layer (a level in a food web). And the less specialized feeders give me barely less pleasure. Thus, as I move slowly along a woodland edge, or through a meadow, or within a patch of scrubby heathland; as I get low to the ground to observe insects feeding on their herbs of choice; as my joy ratchets up towards ecstasy... As all of these things happen, I find my feet, knees, and hands sinking into the soil and my soul being consumed by the habitat. And I find time passing only to keep flying creatures from falling out of the sky.

For other naturalists, the sensation of being swallowed by a habitat might arise from a long series of encounters with our mammalian cousins (as it was for Dian Fossey) or with birds of prey (as with JA Baker), but my personal intoxication seems, for whatever reason, to lie in the touchpoints of small-scale herbivory. This illustrates that a *mutual* emotional awareness is not needed for forging a deep bond with nature.

Before closing this section on biophilia, I will just note that there is also a darker side to natural history. This is the sort of naturalism that burns through a thousand mile's worth of petrol for the possibility of seeing a new species of bird simply to gratify an obsession. And this is the sort of naturalism that involves putting out killing traps to clean the air of insects for the sole purpose of extending one's private list of recorded species. I do not class this type of behaviour as nature love.

Recognizing non-human nature's moral standing

The other facet of my motivation to live in a garden of life rather than one of death is my recognizing of the permeation of moral standing far outside the human sphere. By something having moral standing, I mean that it is a subject of ethical concern *in its own right*. This leads to an obligation for morally responsible agents to endeavour to avoid either harming the subjects directly or preventing them from achieving their interests or fulfilling their destiny. I will illustrate this with some examples.

I am a morally responsible agent in that my actions can be described as being good or bad, ethically speaking. If I punched a human in the stomach without good reason, I would have acted in a morally bad way as I would have harmed that person. For while my punch is not the sort that would interest any boxing trainer, I would at the very least have caused the recipient mild physical pain.

Similarly, if I were to stand by a horse in a field and punch her in the flank just for the thrill of it (if ever the subjunctive mood had a purpose, it was to distance me from that repugnant thought), then I would have harmed her in some way, and with no justifiable cause. She has moral standing and is thus a subject of ethical concern, meaning that my action would reasonably be deemed morally bad.

If, however, I was to walk behind the horse and she kicked me in my own flank, I would not describe her as having behaved in a morally bad way. Rather, I feel that I could only sensibly consider it a morally neutral action, even though I am a subject of ethical concern. (A less charitable person might say I actually deserved the kick as punishment for my own stupidity.) The reason that I would consider such an action morally neutral is that horses—like other non-humans—are not ethically responsible agents in regard to their interactions with other species.

This is not to say that cross-species concern or assistance is unique to humans: there are numerous video clips on the internet that challenge such an idea. But, as far as we know, not even our closest relative of all on Earth, the chimpanzees, can comprehend the complex system of ethics that yields inter-species *responsibilities*. It is for this reason that the asymmetry between a single species having moral responsibility and a far larger group of organisms having moral standing is not intellectually problematic. There is an analogous asymmetry within the human species. A person who has suffered a severe brain injury, for instance, might not be considered morally responsible but would still have moral standing.

In fact, rather than seeing it as problematic, I find it remarkably fortuitous that humans, the only species to ever arise on Earth with the capacity to bring about a mass extinction event single-handedly, are also the only extant species that can engage in the deep philosophical consideration of moral obligations to other species. This quirk of fate might just be what helps apply the brakes to the unfolding grand extinction, although there is a lot of work to do before a foot can be placed on that pedal.

Here's another hypothetical example, this time in the back garden. What if I were to place a coarse mesh cage that was the size of, say, a large refrigerator over a flower bed and I trapped a lone damselfly inside it. Even if the damselfly could get plenty of food inside the cage and had access to a small pot of water for rehydration—and was thus not caused any harm in a physical sense—my action could be deemed morally bad because it was preventing the damselfly from fulfilling their interests, including passing on their genes.

As a final example, what about when I snip off a few leaves of kale to eat? I am causing the plant harm by reducing its capacity to take in carbon dioxide and photosynthesize energy, so should my action not be deemed morally bad, just as I said the hypothetical incident with the horse and the damselfly trap would be? Here the difference is that I feel that I could justify my action. In this case—the eating of kale leaves—I was fulfilling a biological need. As the conservation biologist David Ehrenfeld has written: "Selfishness, within bounds, is necessary for the survival of any species, ourselves included."

Exactly which of our interactions with non-human others are deemed ethically justifiable will vary from person to person, just as some humans find capital punishment acceptable, at least in certain cases, and some do not. In the case of what we eat, a subset of the people in modern societies who recognize moral standing in non-human life forms still find it justifiable to eat meat, but many others consider it unethical. The closest thing to a universal rule that I can suggest is that humans in modern societies *should exercise their freedom with responsibility,* by striving to live a life that is mindful of the moral standing of humans and non-humans alike. Such a guiding principle directly challenges a pervasive modern reality, noted by Eileen Crist, that "as modern freedoms are increasingly disseminated to billions of people, so do the freedoms of uncountable nonhumans become obliterated or constricted."

The extent to which moral standing permeates into nature is also something that different individuals will view in different ways. In order for me to describe some of the main philosophical positions in this regard, I will introduce two new terms. The first is 'intrinsic value', which I use to mean an existential worth of something that is independent of any benefit that humans might derive. I consider intrinsic value in non-humans to imply moral standing, and *vice versa.* The second term is 'instrumental value', which is the worth of something that arises from human-experienced benefits. Of particular relevance to the context of this chapter is that biophilic emotions are purely instrumental in nature. They are a blend of aesthetic and spiritual values that humans derive from the more-than-human world.

A non-spiritual and non-aesthetic example of instrumental worth is the provision of shade to a human by a tree. The tree can also be thought of as having intrinsic value in that its existence has a worth in its own right. Recalling the terms 'shallow' and 'deep' that I introduced in Chapter 1, if someone was to fight to save the tree in order to maintain the shade that it gave humans, they would be doing so on *shallow* terms. If, however, they were fighting to save the tree because of this being's intrinsic value, or the intrinsic value of the other organisms that depended on the tree in some way, then they would have a *deep* motivation.

The following thought experiment, which is inspired by the 'Last Man' argument of Richard Sylvan, will help to further illustrate the nature of intrinsic value (and thus the intrinsic value of nature). Suppose that there is one human left on Earth. For amusement, this person uses a toxic substance to kill all of the flowers that grow in a woodland glade. They wanted to act in this way, and there is no other human who can be negatively affected by their actions. Do you consider what the person has done to be wrong? If you do, then you are recognizing the intrinsic value of the flowers in that woodland glade.

With the concepts of intrinsic value and instrumental value introduced, I can move on to the promised description of different philosophical positions. The first of these that I will describe is called *anthropocentrism*. In this worldview, humans are by far the most important species on Earth, and the non-human world is dominated by instrumental value: intrinsic value is either limited or non-existent. Seeing my back garden as being there entirely to meet the ends of my wife and me would be an anthropocentric position. A more emotive term for anthropocentrism is 'human supremacy'. As Eileen Crist has observed, the latter clarifies the former "via the readily available virulent implications of the idea of 'supremacy'." Human supremacy is not incompatible with the development of green concerns, but such concerns will generally be of a shallow nature, such as preserving 'natural resources' for human use. These shallow interests can be described as *light green*, in contrast with the *dark green* concerns that arise from a recognizing of intrinsic value in the more-than-human world.

I should be clear at this point that to champion dark green interests does not mean that light green interests need be rejected outright. Rather, it calls for a deprioritization of the latter—the shallow concerns. Quoting David Ehrenfeld again:

> Resource reasons for conservation can be used if honest, but must always be presented together with the non-humanistic reasons, and it should be made clear that the latter are more important in every case.

The next position that I will present is *sentientism*. Here the focus is on extending the sphere of moral concern to encompass animals, including humans, who have perceptual experiences such as feeling pain. It is a non-anthropocentric worldview, and its key tenet is striving to avoid human-caused suffering to sentient creatures. In my back garden, a sentientist would be especially interested to see that no harm was caused by humans to the mammals, the birds, the amphibians, and any other organisms whom they considered to have perceptual experiences.

A worldview with a larger sphere of moral concern than both anthropocentrism and sentientism is *biocentrism*. Here, all living individuals, including plants, are considered to have intrinsic value. This value can be seen as arising from individuals having an agency to pursue interests, such as flourishing. In my back garden, biocentric concerns would respect the agency and interests of all individual organisms who live in or visit the place.

The final philosophical position that I will describe is called *ecocentrism*, and it extends the sphere of concern from that of biocentrism in two important ways. The first is by embracing non-living components of the ecosphere, such as rivers. So if a river dries up from excessive abstraction of water by humans, then not just her living denizens but also the river herself can be considered to have been subject to a morally bad action. As Stan Rowe wrote: "No sharp line can be drawn between the living and non-living components of an ecosystem because they are equally important parts of the whole."

The second way in which ecocentrism extends the sphere of concern is by its recognizing of an intrinsic value in ecological collectives, such as species and ecosystems, that is greater than the summed values of the individual organisms. For this reason, ecocentrism establishes a particular duty of care to species that are endangered on account of human activities, which is a duty that biocentric individualism does not. In the back garden, ecocentrism sees a care for hedgehogs, for instance, as having an importance that is greater than it would be from just seeing these animals as individuals with interests, because they belong to a species that is precipitously declining owing to human action. While viewing such endangerment of species as a moral issue in its own right might seem intuitively straightforward, it is in fact an academically complex, and contentious, position, as the philosopher Ian Smith has shown in a book titled *The Intrinsic Value of Endangered Species*. To put it differently, it is a simpler task for ecological ethicists to form a robust justification for biocentric individualism than for the extended sphere of ecocentrism.

Biocentrism and ecocentrism may, in certain instances, lead to differing implications for the way that humans should strive to behave on Earth (I discuss some examples of invasive species in Chapter 8, to which this is relevant). But the differences are not anywhere near as great as their shared divergence from the manifestations of the human supremacist view of the world. And I consider biocentrism as a valid position for what I call an Earth ethic, or a deep green philosophy. (I also see it as a minimum position.) I personally view the world through an ecocentric lens, but I am not out to challenge the biocentric philosophy. The most urgent work that needs to be done lies in combating the idea of human supremacy, not in arguing about different shades of deep green.

For more on the non-anthropocentric philosophical positions that I have described above, including the key literature that underpins them, I recommend Patrick Curry's *Ecological Ethics*. I will just briefly discuss, however, two of the key contributors to ecocentric thought. The first of these people is Aldo Leopold, whom I have already mentioned several times in this book. He was a hunter-turned-conservationist who lived from 1887 to 1948. A pivotal moment in Leopold's transformation to full-blooded conservationist occurred during a deer-stalking trip that he took as a young hunter. His party watched an old female wolf greeted by a half-dozen grown pups with "wagging tails and playful maulings" as she returned to her pack after fording a turbulent river. The hunters—being taught that wolves were bad for deer and thus bad for their hunting too—unleashed a torrent of lead, maiming a pup and killing the old female. They reached the old wolf "in time to watch," as Leopold wrote, "a fierce green fire dying in her eyes." For Leopold, "green fire" was a higher awareness of the wolf's role in her ecosystem—an idea that grew through many years of reflection into his land ethic. In the land ethic, Leopold proposed that the human understanding of community, as comprising interdependent parts, be expanded from a human-only phenomenon to embrace "soils, waters, plants, and animals," and he saw humans as being transformed from "conqueror of the land-community to plain member and citizen of it."

The other key contribution to ecocentric thinking that I will mention here is that of the philosopher–mountaineer Arne Næss. He lived from 1912 to 2009, and his work was central to the formulation of Deep Ecology, a movement that emphasizes the recognizing of intrinsic value in all life. Among his many important intellectual contributions to ecological philosophy was his positioning of concerns for human life as sitting within a broad ecological outlook, rather than separately from it. This is exemplified by the following observation that he made:

> Ecologically inspired attitudes therefore favour diversity of human ways of life, of cultures, of occupations, of economies. They support the fight against economic and cultural, as much as military, invasion and domination, and they are opposed to the annihilation of seals and whales as much as to that of human tribes or cultures.

The interplay between biophilia and an Earth ethic

If standard psychological thinking applies to biophilia and the Earth ethic, then the former would properly be considered as attitudinal and the latter as being a value. Since values underlie attitudes, I could simply speculate that an affinity for non-human nature arises from recognizing its moral standing and draw this section to a close in the first paragraph. To me, however, the interplay between attitudes and values does not fall into that standard pattern. Indeed, I think that biophilic attitudes feed deep green values more than the values feed the attitudes.

I should state that it is not my intention here to disentangle biophilia and the Earth ethic. In people for whom the former has inculcated the latter, it is not the case that biophilia is supplanted or even surpassed by the Earth ethic. The two great phenomena that govern our relationship with other life—one affective and one rooted in the philosophy of morals—work harmoniously. In this way, they are akin to mutually functioning parts of an ecosystem. And like the different components of an ecosystem, they have complementary roles.

One key difference between biophilia and an ethic of moral standing is that the former guides us both in the avoidance of harm and in the enablement of flourishing, while the clear steer that we get from the latter, I feel, predominantly relates to the actions that humans should avoid rather than the ones in which we should engage. Let's take gardens as an example and suppose that someone inherited a piece of land with moderate wildlife value. Here, moral-standing arguments, based on the intrinsic value of non-humans, would create a robust case for avoiding destruction of the life that is there but a weaker imperative to help the land become a wildlife haven. In this way, biophilia, which, here, would motivate both the avoidance of destruction and the enablement of flourishing, can be seen as the more broadly empowering phenomenon in regard to conservation.

Another important difference is that love is more instinctual and thus needs less explaining, while an ethic of moral standing is better suited to underpinning scholarly arguments for the existence of obligations. Relatedly, the Earth ethic has arisen to meet a need of modern society to scale back its deleterious presence, while love of nature has a much more deeply rooted history in the human psyche. To expand on this second point, I am going to ask you to imagine something. The last time I wrote "if you can imagine," back in the previous chapter, I plunged you into an acre of woodland that had just been completely felled by chainsaw. Trust me when I say that the scenario I am about to present is a lot kinder on non-humans.

Okay, then: If you can imagine a world in which the human population has been dramatically lowered from its current size (through, say, a humane, non-coercive approach), and in which an ecological cohabitation with non-humans has emerged as the global reality, biophilia would still be shining as brightly as ever. The imperative for recognizing moral standing, in contrast, would have shrunk, because the ethical injustices being suffered by non-humans would have majorly decreased. As the naturalist John Livingston wrote, "we ourselves created the vacuum into which the need for conservation flows."

A final major difference between biophilia and the Earth ethic is in their differential representation of non-human interests. In elaborating on this statement, I will first mention EO Wilson's attempt to derive a conservation ethic directly from biophilia without an appeal to intrinsic value. In an essay that forms part of a collection on biophilia that he co-edited with Stephen Kellert, Wilson argues for the ethical obligation to conserve wild nature that arises from the "immense aesthetic and spiritual value" associated with life's diversity. He sees the inclusion of these non-material instrumental values as serving to bolster an ethic that relies merely on the "utilitarian potential of wild species" as "untapped sources of new pharmaceuticals, crops, fibers, pulp, petroleum substitutes, and agents for the restoration of soil and water." Without this bolstering, he reasons, wild nature can be "priced, traded off against other sources of wealth, and—when the price is right—discarded." At this point, though, Wilson shies away from also including the intrinsic value and moral standing of non-human nature in his ethic, since he does not see it as providing a robust position. "A simplistic adjuration for the right of a species to live," he observes, "can be answered by a simplistic call for the right of people to live." And intrinsic value, he contends, is "lacking in objective evidence."

Yet, the ethic that he proposes is vulnerable to the same possibility. Someone can always say that economic gains are more important than spiritual and aesthetic values, and since these things lack commensurability, it is not possible to present objective evidence that definitively counters such an assertion. Furthermore, to ignore intrinsic value in the development of a conservation ethic because it does not offer a guaranteed victory is to apply the mindset of a sprinter who forfeits a race before the bang of the starting pistol because other runners have lined up next to her. Most importantly of all, though, I believe that the omission of intrinsic value is a betrayal of the innumerable life forms with which we share a home. Their intrinsic interests should not be discounted from the moral case for conservation since it is not for us to prioritize their conservation according to the values that we derive from them—*even if* such values go beyond the material to additionally encompass aesthetic and spiritual benefits.

More generally, we need to step down from the top of our perceived pyramid of supremacy, and we cannot do this with biophilia alone. Indeed, it is only through an Earth ethic that the intellectual bubble of human exceptionalism can be burst. And, therefore, while I proposed above that biophilia is both a more instinctual idea and a more broadly empowering phenomenon in regard to conservation, I firmly believe that a recognizing of moral standing is needed, in addition, for us to be able to fully honour our fellow Earthlings.

How do biophilia and the Earth ethic apply in gardens?

If you head to your local library, there will almost certainly be a selection of books on gardening and growing food, and some of these will tell you how to manage your plot so as to attract wildlife. If you pull the wildlife-focused books off the shelf and browse the prefaces, forewords, introductions, or whatever else the books have for front matter, you will, I suspect, find yourself reading about the importance of close encounters with wildlife for humans, along with other instrumental benefits such as 'ecosystem services'. I do not dispute that our moral duties to the more-than-human world are often implicitly present in the thought process of the authors, but such considerations rarely feature strongly and clearly in the final output. Additionally, I do not dispute the importance of the shallow benefits that make up the typical focus of the narrative. For one thing, the wildlife that I have been fortunate enough to encounter in my own back garden has had what is a significant nurturing effect on my biophilia. For another, in relation to the growing of food specifically, I happen to share the sentiment of Wendell Berry that there is something of great importance in "making vital contact with the soil and weather on which [one's] life depends." Nevertheless, it seems to me that passing up the chance to expound the case for intrinsic value and ethical duties in gardening books is an opportunity missed.

One work that bucks the trend is Benjamin Vogt's *New Garden Ethic*, in which he proposes that the "challenge before us is to not just embrace shallow ecology as we exercise our biophilia." He advocates, instead, a 'garden ethic', modelled on Aldo Leopold's land ethic, "that links the human and nonhuman, the urban and wild, the present and the future, and binds us to one another as part of a mutually supportive community."

I agree with Vogt that the ideas present in Næss's Deep Ecology and Leopold's land ethic have applicability to our relationship with the garden community, although I do not feel that it needs a special name. The Earth ethic pervades the entirety of the ecosphere, from concrete-covered urban space to the planet's least-touched wildernesses. That being said, there are two things particular to gardens that are relevant to the theme of this chapter, which I will discuss now.

The first particularity of gardens, as compared with the wider landscape, is that they are parcels of land over whose direction individual humans have a great potential power. This is not to say that gardens are the only opportunity for practitioners of the Earth ethic to make 'land management' more friendly to nature. Other ways include buying organic produce, signing petitions, making donations to conservation charities, voting for the greenest candidate in elections, and writing to corporations. But gardens are different in offering an easy opportunity for direct action, even if the results may be relatively small.

The second particularity of a garden is that it is a home which humans share intimately with other lives. Earlier, I introduced Albrecht's concept of *sumbiophilia*—a love of living together with different life forms—and it is in the context of a garden that this must surely apply with the greatest force. In writing this about sumbiophilia, it seems suddenly obvious that there should be a powerful emotional gravity to sharing a home place with other lives. Yet, I think that this facet of biophilia is mostly overlooked in the literature that covers the importance of gardens in enabling contact with non-human nature.

It is worth stressing that the feeling of sumbiophilia is different from a love of mere contact with other living beings. For while connecting with non-humans in the wider landscape can certainly be an emotionally profound experience, there is something uniquely special about sharing a living space. If you hike to some distant forest, find a fallen trunk to sit on, take off your boots and socks, and plant your feet in the leaf mould, the millipede who glides past the tips of your toes is a stranger. If, on the other hand, you sit with bare feet in your back garden, the woodlouse who does the same is a fellow resident. To put it more succinctly, cohabitation represents the sharp end of biophilia.

Of all the aspects of cohabitation of a suburban garden, there is perhaps none that evokes sumbiophilia more forcefully than sharing the food that is grown—just as breaking bread with a fellow human, in a religious or a secular sense, is an action of great social significance. And it is to the growing of food that I turn in the next chapter. ⬡

Chapter 5:
Food sparing and land sharing

Oh it's the sweet cycle of life
Oh yes, it's the sweet cycle of life
Well who am I to complain?
Are we not one and the same?

Lyrics from the Tito & Tarantula song *Sweet Cycle* (1997)

A mong the numerous edible delights that grow in the garden, it is the Sun-sweetened wild strawberries that give me the greatest pleasure (see Figure 5.1). What really sets these apart from the backyard's other consumables is their unmatched sensory exquisiteness. This begins with the aesthetic charm of all those achenes embedded in the flesh's carmine-hued surface; it continues with the delicate satisfaction of plucking fruit from stem; it builds as the potent aroma passes under my nostrils; and it climaxes as I carefully spread the ambrosial flesh across my tongue with my teeth. (Some time ago, in writing a short story, I illustrated the verbal ostentatiousness of an unlikeable character by having him describe various food items as being 'ambrosial', but here I find myself struggling for a better word.)

Figure 5.1: A wild strawberry growing in the garden.

There is another contributor to the joy that I derive from the wild strawberries, and this lies in the plants' self-willed presence in the garden. Introduced years ago, in a 'container', the species has since explored the surrounding terrain with its above-ground runners and now thrives, without intervention, in the cracks between paving stones. In this way, the species exudes potential for the 'future primitive' agriculture that has been envisioned by the writer Gary Snyder, in which food-cultivating practices "go *with* rather than against nature's tendency." As a headline writer might quip: Strawberry yields forever. (Another plant with edible parts that has departed its original container in the garden—in this case by self-seeding—is chives, which I will return to a little later.)

Because of the strawberry plants' self-willed establishment, the pleasure inherent in consuming their fruits is more primal than that mixture of pride and satisfaction that comes from eating something over which one has laboured. The fruits say nothing about me and everything about the Sun, the rain, their evolution, and the soil in which they are rooted. The word in the German language for strawberries, fittingly, is *Erdbeeren*—a literal translation of which is 'berries of the earth'. Only serving to accentuate the earth-given gratification is the greater and more consistent delectability that the undoctored 'wild type' offers over its cross-bred, commercially favoured cousins.

Wild strawberries, for me, are an exemplar of what the nature writer Richard Mabey has described as the "mysterious quality of 'gatheredness' that [clings] like a savour to foraged wildings." This is a quality whose celebration he associates most strongly with the nineteenth century New Englander Henry Thoreau, a philosopher and nature-lover of whom I have already made mention. Appropriate to the present discussion is the following passage of Thoreau's:

> The bitter-sweet of a white-oak acorn which you nibble in a bleak November walk over the tawny earth is more to me than a slice of imported pine-apple. The South may keep her pine-apples, and we will be content with our strawberries, which are, as it were, a pine-apple with "going-a-strawberrying" stirred into them, infinitely enhancing their flavor. What are all the oranges imported into England to the hips and haws in her hedges?

Away from my garden, other local wildings that I especially relish—even more so, Mr Thoreau, than a good home-made hedgerow ketchup—include the intoxicatingly sweet flesh of wild plums on the glorious cusp of over-ripeness, as well as an assortment of leafy flavours, from the citrus tang of beech's spring flush to the bitter garlic hit of Jack-by-hedge. This latter ingredient, I have found, makes a delightful addition to peanut-butter sandwiches (see Figure 5.2). This is a trick that I adapted from Oliver Rackham's suggestion to add ramsons, another plant with garlic-flavoured foliage, to enhance such a lunch. For all Rackham's many great contributions to historical ecology, I am not convinced that any top the importance of this culinary discovery.

For Thoreau, the wild strawberry was a forageable fruit from his home patch that could match the sweet goodness of the more exotic pineapple, even though the precise flavours were not at all similar. The owners of a pub near where I live, in order to offer a more comparable local analogue, sold a syrup that they made from distilled pineappleweed—a species in the camomile tribe of plants that is not

Figure 5.2: Jack-by-the hedge leaves added to a peanut-butter roll.

native to Britain but that thrives in compacted soils and even sprouts out of cracks in the pavement. I have always adored the tropical scent of this plant and once sniffed a flower head so vigorously that I got it stuck high up inside my nose. Being able to enjoy the aroma in liquid form was thus quite a blessing.

On the subject of drinks, the preferred draught of Thoreau, as a proponent of simple living, was plain water. Yet, if he was still around today and was gifted a bottle of pineappleweed syrup, I suspect that he might have been tempted to add a dash to his glass while no one was looking—and to have sipped it with a broad smile.

One other thing that I will mention about the Thoreau passage quoted above is his use of the word 'strawberry' as a verb, in his phrase "going-a-strawberrying." This usage survives in the English language to this day, especially in the States, but it is certainly no longer in common circulation, which illustrates just one of the innumerable connections we had with the wider world around us that have been eroded in the Age of Technology. To my knowledge, 'blackberry' is the only name of a fruit that is commonly used today as a verb in Britain: people still regularly speak of 'going blackberrying'. This reflects the conspicuous abundance of bramble growth in urban areas and the wider countryside (the practice also defies the efforts of supermarkets to tempt residents of Britain, during peak bramble-fruit season, with blackberries that have been grown in such far-away places as Guatemala). The only other commonly used verb in Britain that I can think of which relates specifically to picking fruit is 'to scrump'. Denoting the theft of fruit from an orchard or garden, scrumping is something that occurs on a commercial scale in Britain. Recently, for instance, a large number of apples were stolen from an orchard in my local area that is managed by a charity for which I am a trustee. The story was picked up by a national newspaper—*The Sun*, an archetypal tabloid—and they opted for the rather flippant headline of 'Apple turnover'.

Returning to the wild strawberries in my garden, there is a third contributor to the joy that they offer me, and this comes from the act of dividing their bounty with others, for I am not the only animal who enjoys this delicacy. The same, in fact, can be said about all the humanly edible items that grow in the garden.

The rosemary (mentioned back in Chapter 3) is shared with, to name just one species, the rosemary beetle—an arrestingly attractive insect that has claret-and-metallic-green striped wing cases. Like the plant from which it takes its name, this beetle originated in the Mediterranean region, but it established itself in Britain in the 1990s. As one would expect with a co-evolved relationship, the herb can cope with the herbivore's residency. Nevertheless, the BBC's *Gardeners' World* magazine—to cite just one of the available sources of gardening advice—is happy to endorse the application of neonicotinoid biocides to the plant, as long as it is not flowering and is thus unlikely to draw in pollinating bees to the potential pool of collateral victims (or so their thinking goes).

Continuing round the garden, the raspberries are shared, for example, with green shieldbug nymphs, who suck out the fruits' juices through their straw-like mouth. The sage is home to two rather similar species of diminutive insects with giraffe-spot wings. Their body length is the height of the letter 't' on this printed page, and they are known as the sage leafhopper and the Ligurian leafhopper. The disc-shaped fruits of the honesty—a hot-pepper snack for me—are a favoured food of large white butterfly caterpillars, who accumulate the mustard oils from this and other plants in the brassica family as a defensive strategy against would-be predators. The lemon balm, which I use to give a zero-food-mile twist to various teas from far-flung places, is fed on by the caterpillars of a gorgeous moth known as the lesser yellow underwing. The mint offers sustenance to an equally stunning day-flying moth with amethyst-and-amber wings known as *Pyrausta aurata*, or, more simply, the mint moth (see Figure 5.3). And, in what proves to be a convenient division of interests in the rhubarb, dock bugs and other invertebrates seem to feed only on the leaves, which are toxic to humans, while the stems of the plant are spared for my own consumption.

The idea of sharing plants in this way is not something that features prominently in the typical advice on wildlife-friendly gardening, which, instead, is focused on offering nectar sources for

Figure 5.3: A mint moth nectaring on an ox-eye daisy (more on this plant later).

pollinators, often with non-native plants. This to some extent reflects a bias that exists towards pollinating insects, especially bees, for their facilitating role in human agriculture. This championing of nectar above other dietary specializations of insects is also, I believe, a pragmatic strategy for finding traction with potential wildlife gardening newbies who want to do something to support nature but would rather not have lots of holes and bumps in their foliage. In time, I suppose, they may warm to the idea of such 'blemishes' and even begin to see in them a story of significant life events that have unfolded.

In fairness, focusing on nectar is also a more ecologically sensible strategy for smaller gardens, where it may not be possible to offer food-plants in sufficient quantity, in the right microclimatic conditions, and in the necessary habitat context to support a viable colony of a particular species of insect. In other words, 'commuters' will always be grateful for even a small amount of nectar or pollen, while potential leaf-, stem-, root-, sap-, and seed-feeding residents can be much more demanding about resources. To give an example from the garden, I would be thrilled if the wild strawberries could support the grizzled skipper, which is a locally declining moth-like butterfly whose caterpillars feed on this plant, but I know that this is almost certainly not going to happen. As Andrew Wood notes in his *Butterflies of Hertfordshire and Middlesex* (a local nature atlas that synthesized the recording work of a staggering five thousand enthusiasts), "the conditions need to be just right for Grizzled Skipper no matter how much of its foodplant is available. It is also apparent that creating those conditions could be difficult, even if we totally understood what they were." Unlocking trophic layers is not always straightforward.

I could go on with my description of edible items in the garden that I share with other species. Indeed, I have a pencil-scratched list with a couple of dozen other herbs, fruits, and vegetables, which I had earmarked for potential inclusion here. However, with a desire to avoid my chronicling of this aspect of the garden becoming like a presentation of holiday snaps, I will just give one more example; and it is another brassica.

A couple of years back, I was surprised to spot a grey squirrel making regular visits to a lone kale plant near the French windows, tearing off a single leaf each time and delicately passing it into his or her mouth with both front paws. (I hope that the squirrel was a *she* and not a *he*, as in my mind I will always remember this animal, for no particular reason, as Betty.) In Betty's act of nimble paw-work, it looked as if the kale leaf was moving into her mouth on a conveyor belt, and throughout the time that this was occurring she gazed fixedly at me. All that it would have taken to discourage her was a jiggle of the door handle, but I did not do this. That was because—my reasoning went—I could always go to the shop down the road to buy more kale, but this might be her only source. Clearly, I would not make a good farmer; but then I have long known this.

As a sixteen-year-old, I spent most of the long summer break after the completion of school exams working on a farm in south-east Herefordshire. With its patchwork of woodlands, orchards, and fields, this part of the English countryside retains a bucolic charm, yet there is also a darkness that hangs over it as the place where the savagely violent and brutally perverted serial killer Fred West grew up. Four years before my summer on the farm, the bodies of two of West's early victims had been uncovered in fields a few miles to the north. One had been eight months pregnant when she was killed, with West's child.

Bucolic or dark, though, my focus was mostly elsewhere, for I had got the work so that I could save up for a backpacking trip in western Europe, which I would take the following summer. The prospect of travel was the reason that I was able to stick with it for the whole season.

The work started off well enough, with a few weeks of 'apple thinning'. This was an orchard-based job that involved removing some of the developing apples on well-stocked branches so as to promote the growth of a crop that would be supermarket-worthy. It was particularly important to remove any apple that could be judged misshapen. One common 'deformity'—a small bulge where the stem joined the fruit, not unlike an 'outie' belly button—was termed, for no reason that anyone knew, a 'king's knob'.

I worked hard at this job, and each night, when I closed my eyes, all that I could see were green-and-red orbs. But I did not impress the more experienced hands and, after a few weeks, I was pulled out of the orchard. In fact, only one of the three youngsters working that summer managed to win over the old-timers: a young lady who— in what was my introduction to the phenomenon of colleague-to-colleague workplace feedback—earned the nickname 'Billy Whizz'.

After my mediocrity in the orchard, I was redeployed in the barn for the much less pleasant assignment of 'potato grading'. Unfortunately, this job lasted far longer than had my stint with the apple trees. It involved standing by a conveyor belt as trailer-loads of newly dug potatoes whizzed past, with the task being to remove any unsellable potatoes, along with debris such as golf balls, rubber gloves, and medicine bottles. The rapid lateral movement, in combination with the intermittent stench of rotten potatoes, fuelled a motion sickness that lingered long into each evening. It was also an exceptionally monotonous job. One way in which a fellow farm-worker and I managed to enliven the work was by 'playing chicken' with the rogue objects, such as the golf balls, each daring the other to break first in retrieving the item before it disappeared off the end of the conveyor belt to be sealed up in a sack and sent off to the supermarket. While this introduced elements of suspense and humour to the task, it also led to a far greater number of spurious items getting through our defences than should have been the case.

It was in this second job that I got to know a couple of the farm's full-time employees, who operated the fixed machinery and drove the tractors. I ate lunch with them most days in a small, grubby room to the side of the barn. Some of these breaks were entertaining, particularly the ones in which these two employees spoke of their informal competitive exploits, such as the challenge of getting as long a line of cars as possible to build up behind a tractor by making unnecessary excursions on the local trunk road. Other lunches were more difficult, like the one when a mouse attempted to dash across the floor, only to be smashed into the skirting board by the steel-capped boot of one of the tractor drivers. As I sat there stunned, the rodent-squasher carried on munching his sandwiches as if nothing of note had happened.

There were occasional chances to get assigned to a job away from the potato-grader, but I invariably blew them. There was one afternoon, for instance, when I was set to work in an arable field pulling up rogue wild oats. After less than an hour, the tractor driver who instructed me had clearly seen enough to be convinced of my deficiencies in this task, and I was sent straight back to the barn. In my defence, I had been distracted by a desire to sniff the pineappleweed that grew by the gateway into the field, where the regular compaction of soil by the tractors had created ideal conditions for the plant. In a way, then, it was more his fault than mine.

After returning to school for the new academic year, I got a part-time job in which I showed much more aptitude than I had on the farm: I became a pusher. (What I pushed, I should note, in the interest of clarity, was trolleys.) In this role, I established that workers in this part of the country clearly had a thing for competitions that involved making long lines of items that obstructed traffic. In the case of the supermarket I worked for, the challenge was to push as lengthy a train as possible of the trolleys (*chariots*, as the French more poetically call them). A record attempt was only considered legitimate if it met three criteria. First, reasonably enough, it had to be witnessed by a fellow employee. Secondly, there was to be no use of the strap that management gave us for binding trolleys together (this device was an affront to the art and was rejected, even outside of competitive conditions, by all but one exceedingly square pusher). Thirdly, the attempt had to be made on a Saturday afternoon, the busiest time each week in the car park. The all-time record was a fifty-plus effort by a guy who trained by lifting trolleys off the ground with one arm. My own best was twenty-five, which was not shabby at all (as I said above, I showed some aptitude at this job).

I mention my role at the supermarket not just to brag about a personal accomplishment. In the job, I had access to the entire site, and it was on strolls into the delivery yard, where industrial-sized bins were bursting with out-of-date products, that I first saw what a serious problem food wastage was. Having experienced how hard farm labour could be only months earlier—games of chicken aside—I was now seeing that much of that work was for nothing. And it was at this point in my life that I began to give serious thought to the problems inherent in food production. As I learned more about the destruction of wild nature and the awful conditions that were being faced by industrially reared livestock—and as I developed a deep green worldview—a whole raft of new issues came to light.

The culmination of two decades of subsequent musing is the system of agriculture that is practised in parts of my back garden. As hinted at above, it is not really agriculture at all, being much closer to foraging than farming. And, of course, by being so willing to share the garden's edibles with other species and thus reducing the potential 'yield', all that I am doing, in one sense, is displacing the footprint of my food. More broadly, I am aware that a mass scaling-up of my approach, in place of modern agricultural practices, would mean starvation for many humans.

Such is the size of the Earth's human population that we have no choice, at present, but to assert a claim to most farmable land and manage it primarily for the benefit of our own species. This is a framework on which even organic and biodynamic practices are built. With the current food system, our vast population is propped up on unsustainable and covetous practices, the scale of which can only seem acceptable when viewed through the twisted lens of human supremacy.

Eileen Crist, in the book *Abundant Earth*, gets to the nub of this issue with characteristic incisiveness:

> What must the global population size be in order for all people to be well fed on organic, diversified, and mostly locally and regionally grown food, while also allowing terrestrial and marine species to be freed and rewilded? Simply replacing industrial monocultures with organic production systems, while promoting less polluting and healthier options, would not enable the reduction of land-use under cultivation.

In other words, as long as the human population remains as high as it is—or, indeed, continues to grow towards ten billion—we will be locked into practices that make Earth a human colony above all else. There is certainly real value in changing our patterns of consumption, such as effecting shifts towards plant-based diets with minimal food miles and restricted water needs, just as there is in altering the way that livestock are 'cared for' so as to strip brutality from the system. But without dramatically scaling back our numbers, we will not be able to relax our throttling grip on wild nature. And, in case you were wondering: while technology may help in some ways, it is not a solution in itself. Without a guiding will to shrink the human enterprise, technological advances will not reverse humanity's destructive trend but only find increasingly efficient means of exploitation.

In answering the inevitable question of what a population level is that might enable a mutual flourishing of human and non-human life, Crist suggests, based on available research, that, "from our present perspective, two billion is a sound ideal." And the key to getting there, she argues, lies in "state-of-the-art family planning, full gender equality, and comprehensive sex education becom[ing] part of every society on the planet."

In that last sentence lies what is probably the most important work to be done if the ongoing mass extinction is to be slowed and then halted, thus giving life, including humans, the prospect of a positive future over the coming millennia. In the same vein, choosing to go child-free, or to have one child instead of two, is the most important action that an individual can take to project the Earth from humanity's rampant march. Despite this, the issue of human overpopulation is one that so rarely features in the public-facing work of environment-focused non-governmental organizations.

I will retreat from this big thinking back into the garden now and tie off my line of inquiry into the ingredients that we should be seeking to grow at home. Even if my wife and I set about maximizing our yield of produce, we would not come close to achieving total self-sufficiency: the area of land is too small. In any case, there are many plants in the garden that we cannot derive sustenance from, and we like to employ only the most gentle of agricultural techniques. What we do instead, at least to some extent, is opt for those foods whose true enjoyment demands that they be consumed soon after their harvesting and whose transportation is difficult without the use of wasteful packaging. An exemplar of such a food, and one that thrives in our back garden, is raspberries. I have only ever seen these delicate, delectable fruits being sold in single-use plastic containers ('punnets', as we call them in Britain). Chives are another fine example. They begin to decline in flavour from the moment they are cut, and they are almost impossible to buy without plastic packaging. In addition, with commercially sold chives, you never get their dainty, lilac-hued flowers and thus miss out on the sweet-onion punch of this divine *bonne bouche*.

At the other end of the scale of transportability are ingredients that keep well and that are dense in flavour. Any given area's imports should really focus on such items, especially where they offer tastes that are not available locally. The classic kind of ingredient that satisfies the above criteria is spices, the ancient nucleus of long-distance trade. In my mind, coffee beans also *just* meet the criteria, which saves me the hassle of having to swallow a large dose of guilt with every post-lunch pick-me-up. (If the guilt ever gets too much or if Armageddon happens—whichever comes first—there is chicory growing in the garden, and it is possible, I am told, to make a coffee substitute by roasting its root.)

In fact, I think that I would benefit from a coffee lift right now, and so I will draw to a close a section in which I have offered, if nothing else, a rambling salute to the wild strawberry.

—◇—◇—◇—

Consuming the plant-parts that I have described above binds me to the earth, and so it seems only right, then, that I allow any uneaten parts to reconnect with the soil. I am talking, here, of course, about composting. As Wendell Berry succinctly put it, "a garden is not a disposable container, and it will digest and reuse its own wastes." It will also happily digest and reuse waste from food grown elsewhere, such as the grounds of coffee (further swallowing the guilt). For, to quote John Michael Greer, in his book *The Ecotechnic Future*, "Nature composts relentlessly." The "art of composting," he adds, "consists of setting up the right conditions to put this natural process into over-drive."

For my wife and me, composting is something to which we have rapidly developed a quasi-religious devotion. When we rent a place to stay on holiday, for instance, our first concern is not the existence of a swimming pool or the availability of decent Wi-Fi, but whether there is a system in place for the recycling of food waste. I should say that I describe this peculiarity not in an attempt to imply a virtuousness of character. (My admission above about 'playing chicken' while potato grading should have dispelled any such notion.) Rather, I mention it merely to illustrate the addictive nature that composting has for us.

At home, when we were implementing our own system, we were unable to source the equipment second hand, and so, instead, we set about creating something from old items that were stored in the shed. Thanks to the local council's approach to recycling having gone through several rapid iterations some years earlier, we were left with three large oblong containers for which we had no use. It was a simple enough task to cut out the bottoms of the two that had lids and bury them a couple of inches deep in some exposed soil. The worms quickly found the scraps that we began to add, and very soon compost was being created on site. With the third container, if you are curious to know, we made a new bed of soil, which now provides a home for many beautiful wild flowers—including viper's bugloss, a species with violet-blue petals enwrapping long magenta stamens in flowers that are adored by many nectar-feeding insects.

To the council's credit, when they rolled out some new green wheelie bins for garden cuttings, in place of heavy-duty material bags, we asked if we could stick with the old system, and they obliged us with our wish. I think we must now be one of the final households in the city—if not the very last—using the bags instead of the bins. (I am sure that the people who collect the green waste do not thank us for our membership of the dwindling club.) We have also been able to reach a compromise with the council about the control of 'weeds' on the publicly owned pavement outside our front door. Their standard approach here is to periodically spray herbicides. Following a complaint that I made, however, they seem to have put us onto a special list as they now send someone out to mechanically cut the 'offending' plants. We are normally able to hide some of the growing 'weeds' behind recycling receptacles until they have set seed, and only then reveal them for removal. There's nothing like getting value for money from your taxes.

The reason why we give a proportion of our green waste up for collection by the council, I should say, is that some of it is simply too thick or too tough to be effectively composted in our small-scale approach. The council-collected waste, owing to the much larger amounts involved, can be composted at a higher temperature, and the thicker and tougher materials can thus be digested more rapidly. I have a working hypothesis that the ideal size for a human community is one where there are just enough people producing just enough green waste to run an effective communal hot-composting system.

Not helping our own composting temperature is that we sited the containers in a shady spot. But then—as will be explained in the next chapter, which covers the importance of light—most of the sunnier spots are given over to growth rather than decay. ●

Chapter 6:
The study of sunlight

But the sun, like a lion, loves the bright red blood of life, and can give it an infinite enrichment if we know how to receive it. But we don't. We have lost the sun. And he only falls on us and destroys us, decomposing something in us: the dragon of destruction instead of the life-bringer.

DH Lawrence, from his book *Apocalypse*, first published in 1931

In the same way that we have lost the connection with the natural world that arises from such activities as 'going-a-strawberrying', is it possible that our once-umbilical link with the Sun has also been severed? DH Lawrence certainly thought it had, writing—in the same passage of text from which the quotation above was drawn—the following:

> In the centuries before Ezekiel and John, the sun was still a magnificent reality, men drew forth from him strength and splendour, and gave him back homage and lustre and thanks. But in us, the connection is broken, the responsive centres are dead. Our sun is a quite different thing from the cosmic sun of the ancients, so much more trivial.

I would argue that if the connection had waned in Lawrence's time, then it has waxed again, at least in England. Today, there's only one thing more strongly correlated with the country's mood than is the visibility of the Sun, and that is the fortunes of the national football team. With the football team, in the modern era, specializing in the delivery of heartbreak, the Sun is left to be the chief giver, in Lawrence's words, of 'strength and splendour'. Furthermore, surely there is something in the obsession with sunbathing that could be considered an instinctive pagan 'homage'—maybe even a full-blown act of worship? To put it another way, I do not believe that people with certain skin tones who bathe to bronze their bodies are doing it purely for reasons of vanity. I am convinced, even if sunbathers are not always conscious of it, that they are getting something more out of the experience—and that this *something* is both primitive and elemental.

Just to be clear, there is no derisive undertone to what I am saying here. I really do think that modern Sun-worship is of spiritual significance. Indeed, I believe that it is the strongest emotional bond to the forces of nature that exists in British society today. What's more, with the increasing interest in solar power, the direct linkage between the Sun and our society is only going to get stronger. Of course, one could say that fossil fuels also offer a link to the Sun's energy (albeit from the photons gifted during ages gone). But I would not want to be the person who inspired a resurging interest in crude oil as a means of spiritual reconnection with the sky's arcing fireball.

What about the needs of life other than ourselves in regard to sunlight? Staying with the British context, much practical labour in nature conservation concerns just this. In woodland habitats, for instance, various interventions are conducted in order to satisfy the needs of light-loving plants—including crested cow-wheat and wood vetch, to name just two—as well as heat-loving animals, from heath fritillaries to grass snakes. As an entomology freak, I am very familiar with the need to head to the sunnier parts of woodland in

Britain to find the greatest abundance of insect life, and these days I find myself instinctively moving towards such places, just as many six-legged creatures do. It is as if I am thinking like an insect, except, of course, I am not nearly as good at it as they are.

Conservation-motivated activities that open up the canopy include the creation of glades, the widening of woodland tracks, and the coppicing of compartments on multi-year rotations. A mini-lexicon has actually emerged to describe the various types of incision, including such terms as 'scallops' and 'box junctions'. If you go for a woodland walk and move between brighter and darker areas of the understorey, the contraction and dilation of your pupils will deceive you as to the true extent of the difference in sunlight. Rob Fuller and Martin Warren, in a guide to the coppice management of broadleaved woodland, estimate that there is a twenty-fold differential in the understorey light levels between cut and uncut compartments. The variation is greater still in dense conifer plantations.

Apertures in the woodland overstorey are important in the context of conservation not just because of the large dose of sunlight that hits the floor. Additionally, they offer sheltered microclimates and have a soil layer that has generally been subjected to the deposition of far less harmful chemicals than is the case in the wider countryside. Throw in some decaying wood from mature woodland trees and one has a recipe for a biotically rich microhabitat.

I have a particular interest in this area of ecology; it was actually the subject of the abandoned PhD attempt that I mentioned back in Chapter 2. For my fieldwork, I set about examining the impact of canopy openings on insect communities (see Figure 6.1). Naturally enough, this gave me an opportunity to put a great deal of thought into the light ecology of woodlands. I estimated canopy densities. I studiously measured angles of elevation from the middle of openings to the surrounding trees. And I spent much time considering both the path that the Sun would take through the woodland sky and the shifting shadows that would be cast by mature trees. In addition, I got about as good a tan as is possible in forest-based fieldwork (I am a pagan at heart).

Figure 6.1: The nationally scarce beetle *Gonioctena decemnotata*, on aspen in a canopy opening within a woodland near the author's home.

In conducting this research, there were several personal goals that I had set myself. The first was to not have to engage in any killing of insects, an undertaking that, regrettably, is commonplace in entomological research. There are many species of insect that cannot reliably be discriminated from their cousins without microscopic examination of one or more dead 'specimens' (often, this examination requires the removal of insects' genitalia). Thus, if we want to be able to accurately monitor insect biodiversity, which is an important part of well-informed conservation work, some killing is necessary. Even so, I struggle to bring myself to do this, and so I focus my efforts on groups of insects for which most species identification work can be done on live individuals in the field. Here, I am guided, as much as anything, by the voice of Gandalf in *The Lord of the Rings*, who said: "He that breaks a thing to find out what it is has left the path of wisdom."

There are other cases where the killing is done as part of a methodological need for standardized comparisons, or even just for the sake of convenience and efficiency. Sometimes entire communities are killed by an insecticidal fog, say, just to examine one group of insects. In these cases, all the 'bycatch'—as the collateral victims, *en masse*, are coldly labelled—has died for nothing. Ecological research sorely needs a stronger code of ethics, like that which exists for medical studies on humans.

The second goal that I set myself was to do all the research inside the county where I live, Hertfordshire. If Tolkien's great wizard egged me on for my first objective, it was Jean-Henri Fabre who put me up to this second one. Fabre complained that his fellow nineteenth-century biologists, who seemed interested only in researching the exotic creatures of the sea, "scorn[ed] the little land animal which lives in constant touch with us." (He was hinting, here, at a sumbiophilic outlook, over a century before Glenn Albrecht put that name to the phenomenon.) As the decades have passed, this desire to conduct ecological research in exotic locales has only intensified; yet there are many good questions that remain unanswered on the 'home front'.

The third personal objective for the fieldwork was to do all my commuting to research sites by public transport. As most sites were deep in the countryside, this typically necessitated a combination of multiple bus journeys and train rides, in addition to a long walk. The summer in which I began the work was an exceptionally hot and dry one, which meant that, most days, by the time I had arrived at the site to begin data collection—carrying a rucksack laden with equipment, water, and other essentials (such as a small flask of coffee with which to wash down my sandwiches)—I was already shattered, on account of the Sun's heat. There were other contributors to my decision to stop the PhD, but my lack of fitness was certainly an important factor, and I did not make it into a second summer. Please take a moment to reflect on the irony here: that I was trying to explore how insects might need greater levels of sunlight in woodlands and I could not myself stand the heat that I needed to in order to be able to answer the question.

The day on which I realized that the physical side of the research was too much was an occasion in the summer's burning heart. I had travelled to the most inaccessible of all my study locations, a site that forms part of the county's only national nature reserve. The reserve, in turn, belongs to a larger complex of ancient woodland, some of which has long ago been planted up with non-native conifers, for commercial forestry purposes. One problem with such plantations is that the light levels are so depleted in the understorey that the wild flowers simply cannot survive, even if they could cope with changes to the soil layer resulting, for instance, from the deposition of a thick layer of needles. Many of Britain's native woodland wild flowers have evolved to exploit the burst of solar radiation that reaches the forest floor in spring, before the leaves of the deciduous canopy have emerged from their buds. With a conifer overstorey, there is no such vernal opportunity.

In the case of the woodland complex in question, even more of it would have been lost to coniferization were it not for a forest fire that killed off the young non-native trees that had been added during a later wave of planting. There is a rumour that circulates to this day of how the fire might have been started by a conservationist seeking to protect the community of life of the original woodland.

Returning to the day on which I had travelled to this site, it was an occasion on which that summer's heat was particularly stifling. Weeks had passed with barely a drop of rain, and as I rested in the middle of a scorched glade I noticed how all but the most deep-rooted of plants were wilting towards death. I could also sense a storm swelling...

Right now, I really need to head back to the garden, though, and so I will have to save the conclusion of that story for the next chapter. In teeing up a segue to my backyard, I will first recall the following. At a time before humans had begun to make significant inroads into Britain's wildwood, when wild oxen still roamed the land, natural dynamics, playing out over a greater total woodland area, would have created a plethora of openings for the species that depended on them. Today, though, it has become the role of humans to lead on this work, so as to squeeze additional ecological benefits, on behalf of other life forms, from a limited resource. This does not imply that the woodlands in which conservation interventions are taking place should be thought of as being human-crafted. Rather, as

I have written in a paper in *The Ecological Citizen*, it is more accurate to consider such woodlands as being co-created habitats. In essence, they are collaborations between human and non-human players. Among people with an acutely developed aesthetic of wilderness, such intervention within our wild surrounds is something that might be considered universally inappropriate. (Indeed, I got an email from one such person, after the paper that I just mentioned was published, telling me just how wrong I was to have defended these co-created habitats—even though I had defined strong limitations to my championing of them, which made it clear that I was not advocating a planetary-scale garden. What surprised me was that this was the only angry message I received.) If we are to shatter the harmful dualism of humans and nature as distinct entities, should our biodiversity-supporting impact on the dynamics of woodland, I wonder, not be embraced?

In small wildlife gardens, as in woodland fragments where conservation interventions are practised, we can seek to squeeze ecological benefits from the limited area, especially in regard to the efficient use of sunlight. In what is one of the more typical cases of thinking on behalf of other life forms in modern human societies, all gardeners know that different plants have different sunlight needs. In my garden, for example, knapweed does best in full sunlight, red campion seems to prefer partial shade, while enchanter's night-shade thrives in the dim light under the mixed-shrub hedge. This last species—which, like the other two that I mentioned, is a native plant—has basil-like foliage and delicate spikes of small white flowers. It is the food-plant of a tawny-coloured insect known as a stilt-bug, whose hourglass form and conspicuously swollen knees are, I find, rather charming. Even so, the Royal Horticultural Society, which seems to have it in for almost any plant with the audacity to be able to spread out from its designated spot in the garden (or, at least, one could be forgiven for thinking that), suggests that it "can be a nuisance."

In gardening for wildlife, the thinking on the light needs of plants can be extended to animals as well. For instance, a broad range of nectar- and pollen-feeding insects can be supported throughout the day by a garden that offers flowers of different structures and sizes in each of three zones: one where the morning sunlight is strongest; another where the most light hits during the middle part of the day; and a third that catches the sunlight of late afternoon and early evening. The morning light is the most important of all for insects, especially after cool nights, as these organisms cannot fly until their wing muscles have reached a certain minimum temperature. (All else being equal, darker insects are able to start their flying earlier in the day than lighter ones on account of more efficient absorption of heat.) The early light is especially crucial for those insects who are entirely reliant on their external environment for heat generation—the so-called 'ectotherms'. Other insects, such as bumblebees, can use their wing muscles to shiver and thus generate heat to raise their thorax temperature to the necessary level for flight. This deviation from ectothermy is known as 'heterothermy'.

At the back of the garden, I have carefully positioned pots so as to maximally share the morning sunlight between various nectar-rich plants. I have even gone as far as taking a branch of a flowering currant—a plant that has come into our garden from under the fence—and lifting it up onto a precisely measured prop so as to avoid it shading out a stem of *Salvia*. At the other end of the garden, where the evening sunlight hits, a kale plant that was left in the soil one winter sent several flower-laden shoots up into the sky the next spring. During that season, the kale remained in full sunlight as the plants below it were hit by the shade of the coming evening, and it became a preferred late dining spot for many different nectarivores.

Taking the idea of the kale's upward growth further: in a garden that does not receive much sunlight, a flowering tree can be a gift to insects. In our case, a cherry serves in this role (see Figure 6.2). Before its wellspring of nectar runs dry each year, it truly hums with bees and hoverflies.

It is not just trees that can send nectar up and out of the shade. I mentioned viper's bugloss in the previous chapter as a wild flower that is adored by many insects in my garden. This British native plant does not grow much taller than half a metre. But one of its cousins, which has very similar flowers, has evolved in isolation on the Canarian island of La Palma and it sends its flower spikes

Figure 6.2: A cherry tree sending its nectar up above the early-morning shade.

four metres or more into the air. Known as giant viper's bugloss, or tower of jewels, this plant—according to a report by botanists Arnoldo Santos Guerra and Jorge Alfredo Reyes Betancort for the *IUCN Red List of Threatened Species*—is endangered in its native range on La Palma, where it grows in sunny gaps in the humid, evergreen forest. I imagine that its height was naturally selected for, over time, as it helped the plant to get above the competition for light in these openings. The reason that I mention giant viper's bugloss is because there is one growing ornamentally in a front garden a few roads away from where I live, and I have noticed it to be a true beacon for insects when I have passed it on early-evening strolls. It is not unusual—as is noted on the information labels in many of the world's botanical gardens—for plants that are common in ornamental contexts outside of their native range to be endangered where they are endemic.

Insects are not the only animals who crave solar radiation in a garden. If you live in a temperate region and, unlike me, are fortunate enough to share your outdoor space with (non-venomous) reptiles such as slow-worms, then it is important to know that these creatures, as ectotherms, will benefit greatly from sunny spots. Even some warm-blooded animals—or 'endotherms'—bask in the Sun's rays. There is a fox, for instance, who appears from time to time in my back garden, after scaling at least one tall fence, to sunbathe and doze peacefully in a flower bed. For foxes, receiving direct sunlight in this way on cooler days presumably reduces the amount of energy that they have to metabolize in maintaining their body temperature; I also think that they derive joy from the activity, especially when they feel safe. Urban foxes seem to have an instinct for places where they know they will not get harassed, and it thrills me that the garden can help these beautiful creatures in this way.

All told, in the back garden, my wife and I have strived to maximize the benefit of sunlight for life. In doing this we have had a large helping hand from the other players in the garden. Illustrating this perfectly is white clover (see Figure 6.3). We sowed this one year in a food-growing area that we were resting, so as to return some nitrogen to the soil. (Clover, like many other legumes, has nodules in its root system that house nitrogen-fixing bacteria.) After excelling in its job as a 'green manure', the clover managed to become established within the cracks between nearby paving stones. It now covers several of these slabs, to the delight of a whole suite of nectar feeders. In its behaviour, white clover has proven itself to be a plant that fully embraces the spirit of the garden.

We have also considered the needs of life forms who do not want to be hit by direct sunlight—and not just that delicate 'troublemaker' known as enchanter's night-shade. As I noted in the introduction to the garden, in Chapter 3, there are several cool, shady, moist refuges for animals, like centipedes, who would desiccate, vampire-like, in the light of day. In hotter points on the globe, especially as climate

Figure 6.3: White clover, one of several plants in the garden that has become established in gaps between paving stones.

change ramps up, gardening for wildlife may be more about offering these shady refuges than anything else.

There is one final consideration relating to light in the garden, although it does not concern solar radiation. The consideration to which I refer is our avoidance of using artificial lighting at night, so that we do not harmfully interfere with the behaviour of the garden's moth population. In residential areas, night-lighting, both on municipal land and on private property, is slowly being switched to LED bulbs. A number of papers have been published in recent years looking at whether LED lighting is less detrimental to wildlife than the technology that it is replacing. No clear consensus has yet emerged on just what the impacts of this new type of lighting are. One thing I can tell you for sure, though, is that, like its predecessor technologies, LED lights do least harm when turned off.

—◇—◇—◇—

As a concluding thought, our relationship with the Sun is unique among our ecological entanglements, as a lack of respect does it no harm. The Sun is entirely indifferent to us, and we wholly dependent on it. In stark contrast, as the next chapter will explore, a lack of respect for water can be disastrous for rivers and all the lives who depend on them. ⬡

Chapter 7:
Water wisdom

Mama Nature said
"Can't believe it's true"
Ooh, I gave you life and food for thought
Look, what did you do?
You're killing my rivers
Drowning my baby streams
Day by day by day by day by day
I hear them scream

Lyrics from the Thin Lizzy song *Mama Nature Said* (1973)

"I don't think you respect the drought." That is an accusation that was levelled against a fellow character by Larry David's fictionalized portrayal of himself in the comedy series *Curb Your Enthusiasm*, a programme that is set principally in Los Angeles. Much of the programme's humour arises from Larry's neurotic compulsion to publicly challenge any person who is behaving in a way that he deems to be inconsiderate. In the ten series of the programme made to date, Larry has—other than in his preference for hybrid and electric cars—shown a general apathy towards ecological concerns. But during the latest series, from which the quoted accusation was taken, he has at last brought environmentally unfriendly behaviours—specifically, the wasteful running of a tap—into his sphere of agitation. In California, as in many places on Earth, drought conditions are the new norm. If you ever get a pang of guilt for showing an unabashed happiness about life and wish to be brought back down from your plane, there are few more effective methods than contemplating what is going to happen as the availability of freshwater dwindles and the human population continues on its explosive trajectory. It works every time.

Respect, the word that Larry David uses, is a good term for our necessary relationship with water. *Reverence* is an even better one. The first step in reverence, I believe, is learning about one's local hydro-ecology. To put it another way, I think that many of nature's water woes spring from human ignorance.

In Chapter 2, I referenced a self-assessment quiz that Leonard Charles and colleagues developed for measuring bioregional knowledge. One of the questions that I did not cite—the very first of the twenty, in fact, and one expressed in the form of a task—is this: "Trace the water you drink from precipitation to tap." While we are said to live in the Information Age, facts on the water supply for St Albans are relatively scarce. But then this is not the type of thing to which the typical inhabitant of the area seems to give even a second's thought. Primitive cultures in arid lands would have revered sites from which potable water could be drawn. In the case of modern St Albans, though, it is quite possible that most people are simply oblivious to water scarcity. And for all the mistrust we direct towards politicians, we place a similar amount of faith in 'progress'. A widespread corollary of subscribing to the inherent technofantasy of that faith is an incredulity about problems *not* being solved.

Returning to the city's water, and working from the small amount of information that *is* available, I can say that the supply is pumped up through three boreholes and stored in a large covered reservoir behind a pub called the Jolly Sailor. This is, if only in terms of altitude, the high point of the city. Each of the three boreholes abstracts water directly from a chalk aquifer that lies underneath the city. And the water travels through a network of underground pipes to get from the reservoir to my home. Simple enough so far. What complicates the hydro-ecology is that the aquifer from which the water is drawn happens to be vital for the flow of the Ver, our local river. And the Ver is an example of a globally scarce hydro-ecological entity known as a chalk stream. Taken together, what this means is that unrestrained use of water by humans in St Albans occurs at the expense of a rare kind of river and her wildlife. Seldom are the excesses of humans and the needs of non-humans so directly and clearly opposed.

Nan Shepherd, in *The Living Mountain*, wrote this about her local watercourses: "One cannot know the rivers till one has seen them at their sources." With the Ver—although her historic source, unusually, is inscribed on Ordnance Survey maps—I am sad to say that this is not something that one can hope to see. The old site lies in the Bedfordshire hamlet of Kensworth Lynch (one of the suburbs of a nearby town, ominously, is called California). Adjacent to it there stands a water-pumping station; and so, nowadays, the early miles of the river's course are almost always dry. According to a leaflet produced by the excellent Ver Valley Society to accompany a perambulation that is named 'The Source Walk', the Ver now flows through her topmost stretch only once every quarter of a century, after heavy rain and thawing snow. (And yet the government continues to encourage the building of more houses in the most drought-prone areas of the country with barely a political whisper on the issue of human overpopulation.)

Knowing about the lost life-giving potential of the Ver, I get especially vexed by the wastage of water that has been sucked out of the aquifer. Must people take such long showers in this dirt-free human era? Do golf fairways need to be so green? Must private lawns be drenched daily during a drought? Do driveways (even for people who desire to make their land sterile) need to be jet-hosed so frequently? Must windows be jet-hosed at all, when a bucket of water will do the same job? Do paddling pools need to be filled anew every time a kid takes a dip? And *so what* if a car goes a few extra weeks, or months, without being washed?

Complicating efforts to dissuade people from wasting the water that the Ver needs is the lag that exists between water falling as rain on the ground and moisture reaching the aquifer below. The slow percolation of water down to the chalk strata means that winter rainfall will continue to be made available to the river during a spring drought. So people might wonder why they are being encouraged to watch their water usage during dry periods when they can see that the river still has a good depth. Only later will the drought take its toll on the flow. Only then will fish die for lack of a river.

In some cases, a garden is watered so excessively that the liquid runs off to form large puddles in depressions on the road outside the property. On hotter days, my vexation relaxes instantly when I see birds drinking from these pools. Of all the needs of wild nature, a poverty of water is the one that most strongly rouses a feeling of empathy in me—even more so than does the necessity of finding food and the desire to avoid pain. In a short essay that I wrote for a water-themed issue of *The Ecological Citizen*, I detailed one such potent experience, which happened on a trip to rural Spain that I made with my wife:

Walking late one afternoon down a path that took us from the restored house in which we were staying through the barren and ruggedly pleated landscape, we bumped into a walker who told us of a secret river. More through good fortune than a knowledge of the local dialect, we managed, after about half an hour's exploring, to find a safe descent to the river – a waterway named *el Río Susía* in Aragonese.

Rejoicing in the serenity of this hidden place, I spent some time leaping between the dry patches of the river's exposed slabby bed in search of aquatic life, before the pressing of dusk sent us homeward.

Ascending, we noticed on the otherwise dry track a muddy patch. This natural canvas was crammed with tracks of the river's mammalian visitors: deer of different sizes, the splaying of their slots suggesting urgency; possibly a fox; and almost certainly at least one wild boar, with dewclaw indentations having the wide spacing characteristic of its kind. We skirted the mud to avoid erasing the beauty of the prints with our Vibram soles, as strong thoughts began to cycle... *There were so many prints... The river was not my playground but a vital water source... The mammals must have been thirstily waiting for their turn... What a warm afternoon it had been, and what a tough summer... Why did I stay so long?...* And there it was: a spontaneous, emotionally powerful feeling of empathy for other creatures.

Someone else who recorded an experience of humility that was triggered by a realization of non-human water needs was the novelist Ed Abbey. (I call him a novelist since his fiction writing was the work with which he was happiest, but his essays and travelogues were damned fine too.) In *Cactus Country*, he recalled an experience that he and a companion had while hiking in the desert of northern Mexico in the "awful heat of May." Returning from a climb of a volcanic peak, they passed La Tinaja Alta, the highest natural water tank in the area. Abbey and his companion were out of water with two hours' walking still to go. So they filled a canteen from the natural basin, almost draining what was left. And thus, as Abbey wrote, emerged a dilemma:

La Tinaja Alta is a very small *tinaja* to begin with and this was the dry season. The bees crawled over the damp rim of the basin, bedraggled and puzzled. Now the bird cries seemed forlorn.

Out in the rocks and brush somewhere crouched other small animals waiting for us to leave, waiting their turn for a drink. We didn't see them, we didn't hear them, but we felt them [...]

All the water we had was in the one canteen. We emptied it back into the little stony basin. Not in charity but out of caution. It seemed, after all, no more than a prudent sacrifice to the spirit of the desert.

At this point, I will return to the story of that tough day in the field during my discontinued PhD attempt. If you will recall, I was sitting in the middle of a woodland clearing, where the plants were wilting after weeks without any rain. However, a storm was brewing; and I had no waterproofs. So consistently sunny and hot had the weather been that I had fallen out of the habit of checking the forecast. In any case, my pack was already bulging and there was no space for raincoats or over-trousers. The storm announced itself with flashes of lightning and claps of thunder in the distance, and soon it rolled in over the woodland. After a rapid crescendo from the first gentle drops of water, the rain began to pound violently into the dry earth. I stayed out in the open, as if I had suddenly planted roots. (I was close enough to a tree that my head, which stuck out above the parched herb layer, would not draw the interest of any bolts of electricity from the sky.) My clothes got drenched, but I was not particularly conscious of this development. For I can state, without any poetic exaggeration, that I was experiencing the downpour more as a plant than an animal. The full extent of my empathy surprised me when I reflected on it after the storm had passed through: I had truly relished every drop. For that brief spell of acutely heightened sensitivity to the needs of the broader community of life, all the exertion of the PhD attempt that had gone before it had paid itself off and more.

Back in my garden and home, an empathy for broader-than-human water needs plays out in two main ways. The first is in a recognition of the liquid that comes from our taps for the sacred life-giving resource that it is. The stewardship that my wife and I practise, in accordance with this, ensures that the demands we place on the aquifer, and thus the river, are kept in check. To explain one of the steps that we take, I must first mention another thing on which we endeavour to keep a tight rein, and that is single-use packaging for the food that we purchase. One item for which packaging has seemed inevitable is olive oil, which we have bought on numerous occasions in five-litre plastic containers that have a screw-top opening and an integral handle. (This has been the case even if shopping at a 'zero-waste' store: with oil, filling up the front-of-store dispensers from large plastic containers was for some time the best that the stockist could do. Now, I understand, further improvements to the supply chain are being made by some of the more dedicated shops.) Over the years, we have thus amassed quite a number of large receptacles. Once thoroughly cleaned of the residue of the original contents, we have used the containers to collect the tap water that runs while the flow is warming up. In hot, dry spells, this liquid goes straight into a watering can and then onto the garden. During wetter periods, in contrast, we are able to build up a stock of filled bottles, which we store in the garden shed for use once the weather turns dry again. Similarly, the water used for washing vegetables is saved for giving a preliminary rinse to dirty dishes and then poured onto the garden. It is much better to keep water in its catchment than sending it into the drain for downstream processing. This approach, coupled with the fact that water needs of most of the plants in the garden are modest, ensures that, even in the depths of a drought, we seldom need to turn on the outdoor tap.

Another way in which we reduce our water consumption is by operating a crude system for giving a second life to so-called 'grey water'. *System* is too grand a word for it, really, as all that it comprises is a bucket. We use it to collect bathwater with which to flush the toilet. And, yes, I did write 'bathwater'. While lists of water-saving tips often champion showers over baths, I think that a shallow bath can easily hold its own in the competition, especially if used for the sequential bathing of more than one person. When I was growing up, we needed to watch our water usage in the household so as to avoid overloading the septic tank, and so we had to take baths in the same water, back-to-back (by which I mean in sequence, not sitting in opposite directions). I was the youngest and the fourth in. When I mention this to someone today, the listener typically finds their face contorting instinctively into a countenance of revulsion. Compared with the standards of preceding generations, though, getting any bath on an almost daily basis was pretty luxurious. Part of respecting water in a world with a bloated human population and an unhinged climate will be allowing at least a minor relaxation of hygiene standards.

To this end, I recently completed a six-month stint without washing my hair. (This is another revelation that has triggered instinctive facial contortions in conversational partners.) What I learned from the experience was as follows. First, I did not die. Secondly, my wife did not demand a divorce. Thirdly, I had even more time in which to profit from the great advantage of bathing over showering—namely, sitting and pondering. During this extra pondering time, I found myself returning to the same fantasy: a novel plumbing system that would optimize water recycling in people's homes. This would entail a triple-pipe system, fed by three different plugholes in each sink and bath. One plughole would be for draining almost-clean water into a simple tank for use in the garden. A second hole would be for releasing 'grey water' into another tank, where it would undergo ecologically sound processing, so that it could also be reused on site. A third hole would be for flushing away water that, for whatever reason, the householder did not wish to go into either of the tanks but instead wanted to direct into the sewage system for municipal treatment. Maybe, though, this is just a pipe dream. (Let me guess: your face just did one of those contortions.)

Moving quickly on, I will now turn to the second way in which an empathy for broader-than-human water needs plays out at home. (And I promise to cut a safe path across the minefield of wordplay temptation that results from a central object in all of this being a big butt.)

In the garden, the only standing water—other than the micro-pools that form, like those of bromeliads, in the cups where opposite pairs of leaves emerge from teasel stems (see Figure 7.1)—is the water

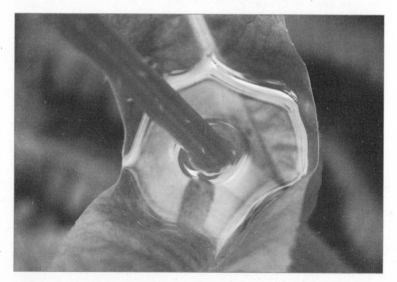

Figure 7.1: A micro-pool of water in a cup formed by the bases of teasel leaves.

in the pond. On hot days, when I see a range of wildlife drinking and bathing in that water, I get a strong sense that maintaining the round-the-calendar existence of this wet hole in the ground is just about the most important thing that I do in my life. The pond is also a source of great joy for me, with this emotion spiking both when there are rare, unexpected visitors, such as grey wagtails (a bird, typically, of running water), and during more predictable events such as the resident frogs' spring chorus.

During warm, dry spells, as the losses to evaporation exceed the gains from precipitation, it becomes necessary, from time to time, to top up the pond. The easiest way of doing this would be to run a hose from the outdoor tap. However, while that water may be monitored to ensure that it meets human standards, I am not satisfied that it is good enough for the pond life. And while I am no water chemist, my understanding is that rainwater is a far superior option.

It is possible to obtain annual reports from the company that supplies my water with details on the levels of some of the different contaminants in the local supply. In 2019, to take just one year, the total level of biocides was found to be above the 'ideal' threshold of half a microgram per litre. This related in part to a higher-than-desirable level of atrazine, a substance that is moderately toxic to aquatic life. Since the use of atrazine has been banned in the European Union for nearly two decades, it is curious, to say the least, that it should be present at such marked levels in St Albans tap water. I know that rainwater is not pure, but it is much less impure, as I understand it, than what comes of out of our taps.

So how can one avoid a reliance on tap water for topping up a pond? Unsurprisingly, the answer is a water butt. There is one in my garden, capturing run-off from the shed. When the barrel spills over, after heavy storms, the water drips down into what has become the dampest area of the garden, where a magnificent fern annually unfurls. (The driest area, in contrast, is the patch of soil under the rosemary bush described in Chapter 3, where an *Andrena* bee had made a den. We avoid watering this patch to help keep the soil friable and thus to the liking of various earth-mining insects. Species attracted to the garden's sandier soils include the ornate-tailed digger wasp, a delicately built but brutish predator with a body of alternating black and golden rings.)

Beyond the occasional need to augment the water level of the pond, there is only one other significant intervention that takes place on a regular basis, and this is the removal of duckweed—a tiny plant that aggregates into large mat-like structures on the surface of various still and slow-moving water bodies, including those as unnatural as cattle troughs. Through the budding-off of two daughter plants from a single parent plant, duckweed is able to multiply rapidly: once present in a garden pond, it can, in the right conditions, quickly spread to cover the entire surface. One has to respect duckweed's fertility. Yet, by covering a pond, the plant eliminates the open water needed by surface-dwelling insects, such as pond-skaters, and it also shades out light. In order to keep this plant in check, in our pond, we simply twizzle it round the end of a bamboo cane and then leave clumps of it to dry on the side of the pond, so that any aquatic life that might have inadvertently been pulled out with it, such as damselfly larvae, has a chance to return to the water. We find this task to be most easily accomplished after a sudden rise in water from heavy rain has lifted the duckweed above the rest of the pond's vegetation. (I say 'we', but this—like the removal of the top layer of soil after the pollution incident that I described in Chapter 3—is one of those tasks to which my wife's far greater levels of patience are well suited.) The intervention is akin to the creation of canopy openings in a woodland, as described in the previous chapter, for it allows light to reach the life below. It is also analogous to the annual scything of a wild-flower meadow, as, like that practice, it pulls nutrients out of the system and thus counters the excessive fertility that can favour a small number of dominant species over the many. In this way, the presence of duckweed actually offers a handy means of safeguarding against an excessive nutrient load. And, with this small piece of assistance, the pond has now found a perfect equilibrium: its water is as clear as it was on the day when it was first filled.

Other than the addition of stored rainwater to the pond from a barrel and the removal of duckweed—the regular activities—only two other interventions have taken place in recent years, and both were one-offs. The first, which I described in an earlier chapter, was the addition of some cut branches from the garden so as to create perches for birds and damselflies and to provide a foothold for marginal vegetation. The other I will recount now.

One evening, a couple of years ago, I arrived back in St Albans on the train from London, following an unexceptional day of pushing a small cursor round a big monitor, punctuated with an occasional tap of the delete key (I mentioned earlier that I work as an editor). This particular day was in mating season—mating season for common frogs, that is—and on my walk home from the station, I spotted a pair of these splendid beings. The duo were locked in amplexus, as the amphibian reproductive piggy-back is termed in textbooks, and they had positioned themselves in the middle of a residential street. Now, I do not intertwine myself in the destiny of other animals lightly (indeed, I wrote a piece for the *City Creatures Blog* on the internal debate that I undergo about where to put snails down after having picked them up off pavements in the rain to save them from being crushed). But I was not about to allow the lives of two frogs on the cusp of reproducing to be pancaked under the wheels of a Range Rover, and so I stepped into the road and strode across to them. I normally carry a plastic box in my rucksack for rescuing any leftover food that I might encounter during the day, and, fortunately, that evening, it was empty and clean. The female frog—the one giving the piggy-back—was most obliging and hopped into the box on behalf of the pair. I loosely held the lid over the container with both hands, returned to the pavement, and continued my walk home. The only safe place I could think to release the frogs was in my own pond, which was about half a mile away (it is not advisable to move aquatic life over any significant distance, as it facilitates the spread of diseases to new areas, but this was a short enough trip to be safe). As well as ensuring that the pair would have a healthy pond for the female to lay—and the male to fertilize—their spawn, this choice of release site would, I reasoned, also inject some genetic variation into my garden population's gene pool.

I got to my house, still clutching the box safely, and I rang the doorbell with an outstretched pinky finger. My wife opened the front door, somewhat surprised that I had not just let myself in. Her surprise became astonishment on seeing that my leftovers box held neither sandwiches nor cake but something altogether more alive. As it happens, British English possesses a most fitting idiom for the occasion. Used for describing a person as being crazy, the expression to which I refer is *as mad as a box of frogs*.

Happily, the frogs remained calm throughout the relocation and were still bound in amplexus when I gently set them down by the side of the pond. I turned to move away, in order to avoid causing them more stress than I already had, and, as I did so, I heard a satisfying plop. *They were home.*

Frogs are not the only amphibians to benefit from the garden pond. This small body of water also serves, for instance, as a wet hang-out for smooth newts. I briefly mentioned these creatures earlier in the book and will now take the opportunity to say something more about them.

Smooth newts, as multi-talented predators, hunt prey not just in water but on land too, generally favouring night-time forays in the latter case (see Figure 7.2). Along with other newts, they belong to a taxonomic family known as the Salamandridae, which also includes

Figure 7.2: A smooth newt, on a paving stone in the garden.

the so-called 'true salamanders'. I used to write tweets that summarized recently published research in forest ecology. While never attracting major interest from fellow users, I found that posts that mentioned salamanders were the ones most likely to be endorsed and shared. Such posts even outpaced ones that covered new findings on iconic mammals such as wolves and bears.

Why should nature-curious humans have a disproportionate interest in salamanders? In attempting to answer that question, I could note that these amphibians are lizard-like in their form and that the lizard recurs as a motif across many human cultures. (All that does, though, is replace the initial question with a new one: Why are humans so drawn to the lizard as an emblem?)

Alternatively, I could tentatively explore a number of other factors that could play a role in this affinity: their characteristic elusiveness; the dramatic coloration of many of the species; the intrinsic poetry of the very word *sa-la-man-der*; and so on. But I will not do that here. Instead, I raise their relative popularity among naturalists to illustrate a more general inconsistency in our awareness of nature's beauty. In aquatic environments, bloodworm midge larvae, to name an overlooked actor, are just as much a demonstration of the primordial soup's creative potential as are salamanders—and they are just as beautiful, too, in their own way.

Aesthetics, in appreciating nature, should never just be about a colourful pattern or pleasing form. Although I tell myself this, I find my jaw dropping to a varying extent when encountering insects of a differing visual strikingness. And I have a suspicion that the bottom of my face would actually detach itself if I were to ever see, say, a Picasso bug—an African shieldbug marked with an outrageously ornate pattern of red, teal, cream, and black. Yet, in its own way, a visually 'plainer' shieldbug from the same family that I can find in my local area is just as exquisite a creature (see Figure 7.3).

While it is the case that I derive a greater aesthetic delight from encounters with some life forms than with others, I find all life equally beautiful. The two halves of this statement are both perfectly true. The inherent inconsistency is just another of life's beauties. That being said, I do urge conservation charities to avoid focusing their

Figure 7.3: A tortoise shieldbug (left) from the author's local area and the closely related Picasso bug (right) in South Africa (photo: Alandmanson [CC BY 4.0]). Is one of these bugs more beautiful than the other?

efforts on protecting and helping the subset of wildlife that provides the 'prettiest' photos for their fundraising leaflets and websites. It is not right to skew life's chances in this way.

—◇—◇—◇—

I return, now, to the theme that I presented at the start of the chapter, which was a respect and reverence for water. After introducing this idea, I made a case for its necessity by presenting a local example of how water usage by humans is intimately bound to the hydro-ecology of a river. I also explored how a deep respect for water can play out, in practical terms, at the level of a household. A broader question that I will now ask is how humanity can better respect rivers at a societal level and, in so doing, show true *water wisdom*. The three concepts that I will cover in briefly attempting to provide an answer to this critical question have potential ramifications that are even broader than the context in which they are discussed. That is to say, each offers a vital pillar in the fight to save as much of the current radiation of life as we can from the ongoing mass extinction.

The first way in which humanity could better respect rivers at a societal level is through a tightening and strengthening of general environmental legislation. Such an approach, through a restriction of permissible activity and a penalizing of violations, would discourage human actions that caused harm to a river and all of her dependent wildlife—including pollution and, potentially, excessive abstraction as well. One campaign working to achieve such a panoramic bolstering of legal protection is called Stop Ecocide. Continuing the work of the late Polly Higgins, it is striving to secure recognition by the United Nations of ecocide—defined as widespread, severe, or systematic harm to the natural world—as an international crime.

A second way in which humanity could better respect rivers is by granting them legal personhood, which would enable them, when done harm, to sue through a human channel. Legal personhood could be bestowed to rivers on an individual basis or arise through legislation that more generally recognized the rights of nature. Grant Wilson and Darlene May Lee, writing in *The Ecological Citizen*, have described some examples of rivers that have already benefitted from personhood. In 2011, for instance, Ecuador's Vilcabamba River, which had been harmed by a road-widening project, won a judgement in the Provincial Court of Justice of Loja that ordered remedial action to be carried out. In this case, the river had qualified for personhood through Ecuador's constitutional recognition of the rights of nature. Six years later, New Zealand's Whanganui River became a legal person, with associated rights, through a parliamental treaty. In the same year, Colombia's constitutional court recognized the Atrato River as an entity with rights and ordered that the government clean up her waters. What such developments have done is to revive ideas rooted in indigenous cultures within modern legal frameworks.

While the ambitions and developments described above are both undoubtedly positive, I feel it important to observe that a bolstering of environmental legislation could be restricted in its application to issues of environmental justice, which concerns human needs only, and thus not cover those of ecological justice, which recognizes all life's needs. Granting rights to non-human nature shares this vulnerability. In the example from Ecuador, the motivation for the case was to combat a risk that the altered flow of the river would harm human riverside populations, while the Colombian case was centred on the need to protect humans from the negative consequence of the river being polluted owing to gold mining and other activities. These examples would thus be more accurately described as 'rights of humans to nature' cases than 'rights of nature' ones. To be clear, the affected people should absolutely be entitled to protection from such human-caused harm. However, the bounds of justice must not be constrained to this limited set of interests. To put it another way, non-human nature should be respected and revered because it has its own interests, not because doing so benefits humans.

Indeed, to extend the bounds of justice, we must go beyond the idea that a positive future for the greater-than-human world lies in a motivation for care grounded solely in human self-interest. Yet so much of the present rhetoric in conservation is designed to frame issues purely in terms of benefit to people. Nature has been rebranded as delivering 'ecosystem services' and having a value known as 'natural capital'. If you try to challenge this human-centred framing in a lecture-hall full of ecologists—as I have done at a number of conferences—you find yourself attracting stares of a kind that I imagine were previously reserved for use against people with leprosy.

I acknowledge, as is the case with the Colombian example, that what is good for humans is also often good for other life forms. And I readily concede, more generally, that it is neither helpful nor accurate to position humans as being in an eternal conflict with nature. This framing becomes nonsensical, in fact, when one reflects that humans, like every other species on the Earth, are *part* of nature. But, as long as an expansionist, human-supremacist mindset retains its dominance among the workings of more powerful nations, then human interests, at a societal level, will continue to clash dramatically with what is right for non-humans.

Let me reason, now, in a different way for the need for environmental justice to be superseded by an ecological justice that considers the interests of all life, including humans. The significant strides that have been made in various domains of equality have not resulted from arguments that fair treatment for discriminated-against groups would benefit heterosexual, white males who do not have a disability (to reference just some of the domains). They have been made, instead, because the individuals within the groups that have been discriminated against deserve to be treated fairly in their

—« Joe Gray »—

own right. It is only, I believe, through the deep-rooted impetus of fair-treatment-for-fair-treatment's-sake that societal taboos against discrimination have been able to emerge with a sufficient strength to shift societal attitudes. So let me say it again: non-human nature should be respected and revered because it has its own interests, not because doing so benefits humans. Only such an expansion of our moral universe will lay bare the lunacy, and the dereliction of duty, that inheres in the ideology of continuing economic growth.

And thus I arrive at a third way in which humanity could better respect rivers—one which would complement the two promising approaches that I described above. What if the interests of a river and her wildlife were considered not just through bolstering legislation and enabling the river to sue in a court case? What if rivers were more broadly empowered by giving them representation in everyday political proceedings—the kind that take place outside of court rooms? What if the river was given a voice and voting rights, via a human representative, within processes for reaching decisions on any issue that might affect her well-being? What if the river's wildlife were also empowered, in the same way?

What if, more generally, democracies could be run on an ecocentric basis? An ecocentric democracy, or 'ecodemocracy', would enact Robin Eckersley's 'all-affectedness' principle, which states that "all those potentially affected by ecological risks should have some meaningful opportunity to participate or otherwise be represented in the making of the policies or decisions which generate such risks." If human societies are to reach the point where a 'meaningful opportunity' for legitimate participation can truly be extended to 'all those potentially affected', then there will need to be a corresponding shift in the dominant view of non-humans to one that respects intrinsic value and moral standing. In the meantime, though, we could make a start by granting representation to at least some non-human players. Even having just a single non-human voice represented in a deliberative process would have the potential to dramatically change the ebb and flow of a discussion.

And why not start with the voice of a river? ●

Chapter 8:
Seeds, 'weeds',
and refugees

We have so far to go to realize our human potential for compassion, altruism and love.

Jane Goodall, from her book *Harvest for Hope*

From grand thoughts on empowering silent voices, the book's thread twists now to a conversation between two men at a garden centre during an English spring. One of the men, who wears a polo shirt that is embroidered with the garden centre's motif, holds a bemused grin. The other, who tries hard but lacks a full complement of social skills, has just asked a question that, it turns out, was inappropriate for the setting.

The person posing the question was me, and what I had asked was whether the garden centre sold seeds for common teasel. The employee explained politely how this plant was a 'weed'. He then elaborated that one would need to be "mad as a box of frogs"—or some similar expression—to want to deliberately introduce it to a garden. "So that's a 'no', then?" I responded, digging deep to match his civility. (I have taken a couple of pops at the Royal Horticultural Society in this book, but I happily report here, in the spirit of balance, that the organization, on its website, gives a thumbs-up to common teasel, for its biodiversity-supporting benefits.) In the end, I waited till the autumn and collected some wild seed from several teasels growing on the south bank of the Thames in London. When gathering wild seed, it is advisable to do the collecting from several non-neighbouring plants. This adds to the genetic diversity of what you will be sowing, and it ensures that you do not take too many sparks of new life from any one spot and thus hamper the chances of the plant's successful self-seeding there.

The teasels from which I collected seeds were ones that I had passed on a walk before work. I was following a route which, at that time, I took habitually on mornings in Central London. As I took these strolls, I wrestled with various puzzles, such as why I was wilfully and regularly travelling to a place that was at once so crowded and so lifeless. Several years on, teasels are now well established in the garden, offering food and a home to a variety of invertebrates, and also—along with knapweed—providing winter sustenance for goldfinches, who tweeze these plants' seeds out with their thin bills. (Meanwhile, I am no nearer to solving that puzzle.)

One need not collect wild seed at all, of course. In Britain, there are numerous suppliers who sell seed which has been harvested from organically grown native wild flowers. My wife and I have bought such seed from online suppliers—for many plants, this is the only means for their procurement—and there are surely few things better suited to being sent in the post. Kilograms of biomass is locked up in a few grams of potential, with no need for unecological packaging. In this way, seed is like spice. (This is a type of ingredient, as I noted in Chapter 5, on which long-distance trade should be focused, within an ecological civilization.)

In choosing which seeds to sow, the nature of the soil, rainfall, and sunlight may all be important factors in determining the wild flowers that are most likely to thrive. Offering a good guide are the species that already do well in comparable situations within a local area. Since the occurrence of these plants might mean that at least some of the invertebrate species that they can support are also present locally, their addition to a garden may prove to be particularly beneficial for biodiversity. Here, I am thinking beyond pollen and nectar feeders to those invertebrates with life stages, such as caterpillars, that depend on nutrition from leaves, stems, roots, or seeds.

Nectar, while an energy-rich resource, is often made readily available by plants as part of their reproductive strategy. Where a challenge is presented to would-be nectarivores, such as by enclosing nectar sources inside long thin tubes of petals, this will serve to benefit the plant in some way, such as through helping ensure the receipt or transfer of pollen. (I wonder if plants, by encouraging specialization in nectarivores on an evolutionary time-scale, may also gain a benefit from attracting visitors who feed on a smaller range of flowers than a generalist would and who thus more frequently visit plants of the same species and facilitate pollination with an increased likelihood.)

In contrast, internal fluids and the tissue of leaves, stems, and roots are not so generously sacrificed by plants. When these things are fed on, the plant suffers losses to its energy reserves, to its photosynthetic capacity, or to its nutrient- and water-sequestering potential, and it also becomes susceptible to infection—all without any upside. Unsurprisingly, then, many plants exhibit defensive ploys against such herbivory. Their strategies can be chemical or mechanical. They can also be a combination of the two, like with the common nettle, which has stinging hairs that secrete inflammation-inducing chemicals. Or, as described in a paper by Kathy Williams and Lawrence Gilbert that was published in *Science*, they can be even more devious. Certain species of passion-flower have evolved the ability to produce structures that are similar to the yellow-coloured eggs of heliconian butterflies. Williams and Gilbert reported that female heliconian butterflies who were searching for a host on which to lay their eggs tended to overlook plants that had already been laid on—so as to avoid competition—and also tended to skip plants that had no eggs on them but that bore the egg-mimicking structures.

Seeds present an intermediate case between nectar and plant tissue. In some cases, plants encourage their consumption by enclosing them in a nutritious package, as a strategy to facilitate their dispersal. In other cases, the activity is disadvantageous to the plant. Most seed feeding by insects falls into the latter category.

All told, defences against herbivory can be sophisticated, and sometimes fierce, and a degree of specialization is often needed to overcome them. Many herbivorous invertebrates thus have a strong preference for a select group of plants to which they are well adapted and, in extreme cases, they may be dependent on a single host species. While wildlife gardeners might be tempted, accordingly, to introduce as diverse a range of plants as possible, to the point that each species is present as just one or a few individuals, it is probably better to be less ambitious in this regard. As was touched on in Chapter 5, a decent-sized population of a particular plant species might be necessary in order to attract and support its specialist feeders. The number that constitutes a 'decent' population is something that, to a certain extent, will depend on the size of the plant. A lone oak, for instance, can support many different species, but a single grass plant may not attract many graminivores.

When working with a small wildlife garden, then, one will be faced with difficult choices about plant selection. My personal recommendation is that, as well as trying to offer a diversity of flower structures and sizes to support a broad range of nectar and pollen feeders, it is probably best to focus on a more restricted range of food-plants for other herbivores, so that there is space for each to become established in some number. That is not to say that a small patch of a plant cannot attract associated herbivores. In my backyard, a clump of a succulent-leaved plant known as stonecrop that is no larger, in its total extent, than the palm of my hand has become home to a population of an insect that feeds on it. The only established name for this particular herbivore is its scientific one, which is *Chlamydatus evanescens*. If that seems a bit unwieldy, let me first note that this moniker is more easily remembered and regurgitated than that of an oak-dwelling family-member that goes by the name *Dryophilocoris flavoquadrimaculatus*. (I admit not only to a secret pleasure in pronouncing those fourteen syllables with well-rehearsed ease in front of a small crowd on nature walks, but also to making special detours to mature oak trees so as to engineer the opportunity. This is about as close as one can get to showboating during such an activity.) In the case of the stonecrop denizen, which is dark, diminutive, and commonly encountered around old gravestones, the entomologist Rob Ryan has proposed a vernacular name for the species: the undertaker bug. Until Ryan began poking around in graveyards and encountering formerly unknown populations, this insect was considered to be rare in Britain.

In my backyard, the more abundant species of plant include red campion, ox-eye daisy, and forget-me-not, and each has attracted its own insects to the garden, besides nectar feeders. Starting with the first of these, the campion has drawn in a small, elongate species of plant bug in the genus *Dicyphus*. This bug, while having a close association with campions as a go-to food source, also dabbles in predation. Two of this plant bug's closest relatives have also been drawn in. One has come in to live on the foxgloves. The other has been attracted by several greater willowherbs, which have colonized the pond, having gained a foothold on the dead branches that I added with this possibility in mind. This chain of developments, of course, gave me much pleasure.

Willowherbs, in general, are prolific colonizers, a trait aided by the masses of downy seeds that they produce, which float on the lightest of winds. Rosebay willowherb, for instance, is well known for its ability to fill newly created woodland clearings with its stems. According to Richard Mabey, the presence of large stands of this plant used to interfere with fox hunting in Britain as the seeds would get up inside the noses of the hounds and hinder them from scenting the prey that they had been directed to track down. While it is unfortunate that the hunting dogs had to endure what was presumably a discomforting experience, I like to imagine that the phenomenon was a woodland's way of protecting her foxes.

Returning to my list of three of the more abundant plants in the garden, I have a lot to say about the second species, and so, for fear of overlooking the third and failing to heed the wish expressed in its name, I will comment on that one now. Specifically, I was delighted to find a forget-me-not shieldbug in the garden, for the first time, while writing this book. Belonging to a family known as the burrowing bugs, this glossy black species has robust spines on its legs to aid with digging earth, and it spends much of its time at the base of forget-me-not plants or in the soil below. That being said, bugs of this species are known to climb up forget-me-not stems to feed on the seeds, and they are even occasionally sighted high up on a plant while it is still flowering (see Figure 8.1).

And so I come to ox-eye daisies. Many wildlife gardeners will have a species of plant that they champion above all others for its special value in supporting a diversity of life in their particular locality, and this is mine. In late spring and early summer, these daisies suck in invertebrates like filings to a magnet. Across approximately two hundred flower heads—or 'capitula' as they are called with daisies—I have seen, at a single point in time, representatives of all of the five most species-rich insect orders on Earth: the beetles (Coleoptera); the true flies (Diptera); the moths and butterflies (Lepidoptera); the wasps, bees, and ants (Hymenoptera); and the true bugs (Hemiptera). Furthermore, taking the most speciose order of that quintet, the beetles, I have simultaneously observed members of five families: the false blister beetles; the larder beetles; the sap beetles; the ladybirds; and the longhorn beetles. In the case of the last of these families, the insect in question was the fairy-ring longhorn beetle (see Figure 8.2), a species whose vernacular name refers to its larval habit of fattening up below ground on fairy-ring champignons.

Figure 8.1: A forget-me-not shieldbug, one of many species present in the garden. (This photo was taken at a nearby nature reserve.)

Figure 8.2: A pollen-covered fairy-ring longhorn beetle on an ox-eye daisy flower head. (If anyone ever tells you that bees are the only pollinators, please show them this photo.)

The fungus on which the fairy-ring longhorn beetle feeds is one that grows beneath lawns and other close-cropped grassy habitat, often developing into a large circular form. "Rings come about," according to the mycologist John Wright, "when the underground cotton wool-like mycelium of the fungus grows outwards from a central point and dies off in the middle." Individual fungi of this species, he notes, "can live for a thousand years and grow up to half a mile across." Even without the presence of above-ground mushrooms, the fungus's form is apparent in a band of lush grass where the soil has been enriched with nitrogen. A recent notable appearance of fairy rings in Britain was in the middle of Lord's cricket ground, where the fungus slowly digested decaying matter, and offered nutrition for longhorn-beetle larvae, as the youthful Jofra Archer bowled England to a first World Cup title. But, as tangent-prone writers are wont to say, I digress.

Returning to the ox-eye daisies, I could spend an hour or more contentedly watching the comings and goings on their capitula, so abundant and rich is life atop them. I would like to be able to give a good name to this pastime and am currently seeking an improvement on my opening effort: 'capitulating'.

I am not the only being in the garden alert to the special allure of this species. Flower crab spiders wait on the daisy heads to ambush prey (see Figure 8.3). Females of this spider are able to change their body colour, over a period of several days or longer, between white, pale green, and yellow. In the case of the ox-eye daisy, they opt for a white coloration so as to be camouflaged against the outer florets.

Another visitor to the ox-eye daisy's capitula has been an insect known as the broad-blotch drill moth, whose caterpillars feed on the plant's roots, showing that the flower heads are not the only attraction of this plant for other life.

There is something even more rewarding than watching wildlife being drawn into the garden by the plants that my wife and I have had a hand in introducing, and that is observing the same thing happen with natural colonizers. To give an example of such a chain of events, grey squirrels have, over the years, buried numerous hazelnuts in the backyard, which, I presume, they collected from a heavily fruiting tree a few houses away. As a result of the squirrels' failure to recover all of their buried stores, there are now five healthy hazel saplings growing in the garden. Furthermore, the saplings

Figure 8.3: A crab spider lying in wait for prey on the head of an ox-eye daisy.

have attracted a small, elongate insect with a dark body and pale appendages. Like the stonecrop bug, this species lacks an 'official' vernacular name, but—inspired by Rob Ryan's effort, and thinking of a coffee that is black with white froth—I shall tentatively name it the hazel macchiato bug.

In order for the hazel macchiato bug to make a home in the backyard, all my wife and I had to do was avoid yanking some growing saplings out of the ground. Wildlife gardening need not be difficult or arduous. Similar unguided developments to this establishment of hazel include, in recent years, the sprouting of a birch seedling, as well as the emergence, on the edge of the garden, of a holly sapling. The seed for the former probably arrived on the wind, and, for the latter, in a dropping from a bird perched on the fence. Both of these species, like hazel, will trigger a cascade of life-enriching events.

As noted back in Chapter 3, my wife and I are welcoming of plants that establish themselves in the garden—or 'weeds', in common parlance. Our *unorthodox leniency* here is part of embracing the wild forces of nature: that most potent nourisher of beauty. Indeed, while weeds could be considered, through a shallow analysis, as antithetical to the wild, quite the opposite is true. They help ensure that wildness pervades even the most hostile of places—from "a bombed city" to "a crack in the wall," in the words of Richard Mabey. As well as being agents of nature's wild power, weeds should be seen as our friends too. They are the plants that insist on thriving in human company, benefitting from us "when we stir the world up" and "disrupt its settled patterns," as Mabey has put it. They are the plants "that green over the dereliction we have created." And, while we persecute them in our gardens, on our pavements, and down our alleyways, they are the plants that come back year after year after year.

The unorthodox leniency of my wife and I means that, even if the plot were much bigger, our backyard would never be considered appropriate for being shown as part of a society's programme of 'open gardens'. It is, instead, the type of garden that tidy-minded enthusiasts would, depending on their level of charity, either walk past as quickly as possible, tutting all the way, or just gently shake their head at while issuing a sympathetic sigh. *Who,* they might ask, *are the people responsible for this? And, oh my, have they actually let their plants go to seed? How monstrous! Those things could just spring up anywhere next year.*

But then 'tidiness' and 'death' share a root source in Latin. Okay, that last statement is not true, but it would be make my point marvellously if it was, because an obsession with tidiness and control can be fatal to a garden's chances of wild vigour and biological richness. Such an obsession also stamps out much of the potentiality for surprise and wonder. Conversely, if one is prepared to loosen one's grip on a garden's course, it will tend to vibrancy. In our case, I have been truly stunned by the diversity of insects that have found their way to the garden. And with each additional year of wildness accrued, the garden attracts and nurtures yet more life.

I should note here that the unorthodox leniency is something that my wife and I extend to the exotic plants that have colonized our garden. And, so, when my wife and I do cut back plants to ground level or pull them out—roots and all—it is normally a non-discriminatory act, targeting an individual not because of its appearance or its identity but simply because it is, for instance, obstructing a pathway. I say *normally.* I have my eye on a cotoneaster, which is a non-native berry-producing shrub that is growing in an old ceramic container, having presumably entered the pot in a bird dropping. This plant can be a problematically invasive species (by 'invasive', I mean a species that has the potential to become dominant to the detriment of already-present species), and once it starts to bear fruit, it will be prone to onward spreading via the route by which it arrived.

I should say that if you're not sure how to pronounce this plant's name, it is *kur-toe-nee-aster,* with the *toe* emphasized. I wish that someone had told me this when I first read it. I must have ended up mispronouncing it as *cotton-easter* on three or four separate occasions before someone was kind enough to put me right. The thing was, I actually knew that there was a word pronounced *kur-toe-nee-aster.* My parents had talked about this plant when I was growing up. It is just that when I read 'cotoneaster', I was somehow unable to make the link. But then at least I am not alone in this. Because so much transmission of information in natural history is done via text rather than speech, conversations during nature walks are littered with mispronunciations. If you are alert to someone's verbal slip, you can notice the subtle eye flicks of the people who are in the know as they process whether it would be kinder to help the person out or to say nothing. Mostly people stay quiet.

The principal reason that I raise cotoneasters is not to make a point on the behavioural ecology of natural historians but to illustrate how a small but significant part of wildlife gardening is avoiding certain non-native plants—from bamboo to three-cornered leek, in the British case—that could be detrimental to overall biodiversity if they escaped into the countryside. Do not assume that because a plant is on sale in a garden centre, it is okay. Plants to avoid, at least in Britain, include the much-touted butterfly magnet that is buddleia. Unless you source a cross-bred variety of this plant that is sterile or are disciplined about pruning all of the flowers before they set seed, this is a species that can cause problems if, for instance, it spreads into a woodland. To be clear, it would be folly to attempt to eradicate the plant, and it is difficult not to admire its lifesome spread along railway lines and into industrial wastes. But there seems to be no sense in exacerbating the issue.

The need to be careful about avoiding alien plants that are potentially invasive is especially true where a property is situated near good wildlife habitat. Indeed, a key problem with new housing developments that abut important wildlife sites, such as old woodland, is that the residents tend to throw their garden waste over the back fence. And green waste—in its potential triggering of new life through seeds, bulbs, and other plant parts with reproductive possibility—can be so much more damaging than plastic and metal.

Although my wife and I are hemmed in by suburbia, we are nevertheless attempting to keep in check our garden's bluebell population. These flowers are a hybrid between a British native species and an Iberian species, and, if they were to escape, this would be potentially detrimental to the gene pool of the pure native. Where plants such as these are pulled up, it is advisable not to add them to the compost pile, as they could easily sprout again from wherever the new soil is placed.

While alien species that behave as weeds are often vilified, and sometimes even demonized, it is good to remember that they are entirely innocent: their presence in a place can be attributed always to human agency (by the very definition of 'alien' in ecology) and often, specifically, to human carelessness. At the same time, alien weeds have had champions over the years. Richard Mabey states that the Irishman William Robinson, who lived from 1838 to 1935, was the first authority to suggest that the "feral beauty of weeds" might have a place in British gardens, and in this he had a penchant for exotic plants. Robinson's vision for gardening was one "in which plants were allowed to mingle with each other as they did in nature." For he was an admirer—notes Mabey, quoting the Irishman directly—of the "mystery and indefiniteness that constitute beauty of vegetation in its highest sense." On a more practical level, Robinson played a significant role not just in popularizing certain species that are now problematic invasive plants in Britain, such as Japanese knotweed, but also in promoting an approach to gardening that, ultimately, facilitated their escape 'over the wall'. Today, conservation organizations, government bodies, and private landowners all find themselves having to undertake expensive and labour-intensive programmes in order to control invasive alien species.

Thinking at the level of a landscape, it might well be a prudent course of action to seek to eliminate alien species where their presence is likely to be of significant detriment to native biodiversity, as is the case with cherry laurel, to name another invasive shrub. In many instances, though, it is not. It would be hard to argue, for example, that British ecosystems are being impoverished by green alkanet, say, even though it is an alien. More generally, attempting to eliminate a non-native species is not without potential ethical problems, especially in the 'lethal control' of animals—such as, to give just one case, the coypu (a beaver-like semi-aquatic South American mammal) in France and elsewhere. Here, a golden rule for the authorities should be to seek to exhaust humane, non-lethal methods before entering into a programme of death, and only then to do so if it seems likely that it will not ultimately be futile. Furthermore, we should always mourn those who die, lest we devalue their lives and become blasé about such killing.

Let's return, now, from the discussion of potential escapees to look again at the ways in which plants can enter a garden. Another route by which plants have arrived in our backyard is under the fence. The previous neighbours on one side owned their house for several decades and were proud of their garden. It was home to a diversity of plants and they kept it free of toxic substances. New neighbours came in, though, and opted for a simpler garden, comprising not much more than a monoculture lawn (a mercy was that it was a living monoculture, not a plastic simulacrum). On the day that most of the plants were ripped out, a wave of life forms fled to find refuge in our backyard. Among the insects disturbed by the works was a lesser stag-beetle, which is another of those species that has a scientific name well suited to showboaters in possession of a fluid tongue: *Dorcus parallelipipedus.*

At least one plant survived the garden conversion, and that is a shrubby species known as tutsan that crept in under our fence before it was too late. As a resident of the city of St Albans, I feel a heightened obligation to refugees of all kinds, for a reason that I shall now explain. The city is named in honour of Alban, the first recorded British Christian martyr, who is thought to have been executed there around the end of the third century of the common era. Alban, the story goes, was a pagan and an ordinary man who gave refuge to a Christian priest fleeing persecution. The piety of the priest observed by Alban while he was sheltered inspired the host to convert to Christianity. When the authorities tracked the priest down, Alban presented himself in his guest's clothing so as to be arrested in place of him. It quickly became apparent what Alban had done, and he was sentenced to the punishment that the priest was due to receive—unless the new convert refuted Christianity, which is something that he would not do. Thus, Alban was tortured and then, after enduring that resolutely, was sentenced to beheading. Among the feats that have been attributed to Alban on the day of his death was the drying up of the Ver to allow the execution party to cross the river and thus hasten his arrival at martyrdom. (Today, with the heavy level of abstraction, there would have been less need for this.) According to the website www.catholic.org, which I am led to believe is a pukka resource, Alban is recognized as the sole patron saint of refugees and one of a handful of patron saints for converts and for torture victims.

Staying with the theme of non-human refugees, Britain is likely to receive a wave of insect species fleeing north over the coming decades as climate change makes certain habitats in continental Europe less habitable. The island, therefore, has an obligation, I believe, to ensure that there is an abundance and diversity of good-quality habitats that are available, with good connectivity between them.

Life in the deep green neighbourhood: Closing remarks

I will draw this section of the book to a close with some brief overarching remarks. The first thing that I want to note here is that my wife and I started out with almost no practical experience and little in the way of knowledge. Even now, we consider the expertise that we have developed to be limited in its scope to one small backyard in a suburb of St Albans—a garden which still has a habit of surprising us. As I imagine is the case for most people who care about a garden, we are just feeling our way as best we can, trying to make sense of often-conflicting advice; and, from time to time, we experience setbacks. This is true of what we do for the pond, of our choice of plants, of our interaction with the soil, and of everything else.

At the same time, I do not want to imply that gardening for wildlife need be excessively complex or arduous. That is not the case with digging a pond (an act for which robins will thank you both immediately, on account of the liberated worms, and later, many times). Nor is it the case with scattering native seeds. Or with piling up dead wood and leaves. Or with avoiding toxic substances. Or with ensuring that small land-based creatures can get in and out. Or with sitting back and watching the arrival of birds, bats, bugs, bees, bush-crickets, and beetles of wondrous variety.

And you do not need to be an expert in identifying the different species that arrive. You will be able to appreciate an increase in biodiversity even without putting names to all of the creatures. This will be one of the most important signals that the garden will send you. With this, as with the other signals, it is important to listen to what is being said.

And so gardening for wildlife falls comfortably between the extremes of 'effortless' and 'onerous' and, in this, it is a deeply enjoyable and rewarding experience. Personally, I am proud of my role in the life of the backyard as much as one can be proud of anything where the vast part of the creativity lies in the work of beings other than oneself, and where one's main contribution is to leave other agencies to flourish along their own paths. But then respecting, and revelling in, the agency of others is the essence of my belonging in the deep green neighbourhood. ⬡

Part three

Mysteries, travel, and celebrations

Chapter 9:
Mysteries of life

Those who dwell, as scientists or laymen, among the beauties and mysteries of the earth are never alone or weary of life.

Rachel Carson, from her book *The Sense of Wonder*

In Part Two, I plunged head first into the core issues for life in my backyard, as experienced by someone who holds a deep green worldview. Here, in Part Three, I offer a series of lighter vignettes that—by recounting some of the other experiences that I have had in the garden—expand on this theme and touch on other green issues.

—◇—◇—◇—

There are few things that natural historians relish more than the satisfaction of knowing the name and the rough ecology of the species that they encounter when in the field. Something that does trump this is happening on an unexpected occurrence that is far enough outside one's ken to infuse the task of identification with the wondrous quality of mystery. As I recently learned, this can take place on a piece of land as familiar as one's back garden.

The mystery began one night, a few years back, when I was walking along a pavement a couple of streets away from my home. On this particular night, I became suddenly conscious of noises that I had been hearing for some time on evening strolls without giving them dedicated attention. The sounds, now that I was listening to them properly, had an exotic quality to them. My first thought was that someone might be keeping a tropical bird or frog in their garden. But then they were not coming from just one property: there was a chorus of animals singing from near and far.

I walked on and did not give the puzzle too much more thought until the next summer, when the sound reached our garden. Now it was less of a chorus and more of a lone voice, and, with the opportunity to study it in isolation, it struck me that the sound was rather like the periodic beeps of a smoke alarm's low-battery alert. With our curiosity piqued, we tried to locate the source of the noise. My wife became convinced that the sounds were emanating from beneath the soil. As the more experienced naturalist in the couple, I dismissed this as being a far-fetched idea; but I got no nearer to locating the singer. (A friend who is a birder suggested that I might have a scops owl in the garden. This, it turned out, was a birder's version of a joke: scops owls cannot be found in Britain.)

That winter, another mystery began to unfold in the garden, this time in the pond. I was staring into the water and noticed that there were still tadpoles in there, which was strange because they should all have passed through the froglet stage by then. Moreover, these wrigglers were gigantic (by tadpole standards). I wondered if, under certain conditions, common frog tadpoles might overwinter and, in so doing, reach a much larger size than they normally did. I mentioned the occurrence, and my hypothesis, to a number of experienced naturalists. All agreed that it was an interesting observation, but no one could suggest what was going on. So now I had two mysteries and not a hint of a solution to either.

The following summer, I was carrying out an invertebrate survey at a nature reserve in my area when I happened to mention the beeping sound to a new member of our recording group, who was monitoring arachnids. "You've got midwives, mate," he casually responded. And thus were both mysteries solved.

The species to which he was referring was the common midwife toad (see Figure 9.1). Although the adults have a warty skin, this amphibian is technically a frog rather than a 'true toad'. Mature individuals barely pass five centimetres in length and are thus much smaller than fully grown common frogs and common toads, which are species that also live in the garden. But the overwintering larvae of the midwife toad reach a substantially greater size than those of the other two species, hence the oddly large tadpoles in the pond.

Female midwife toads lay strings of eggs, which the male fertilizers and then wraps around his hind legs. He will carry these until the tadpoles are ready to hatch, a behaviour for which the species got its common name, as well as the second part of its scientific binomial, *Alytes obstetricans*. The beeping calls, I should note, are also part of the mating behaviour of the species. Jean-Henri Fabre, living in a time before smoke alarms, spoke of the sound as being like a tinkling bell, which is a delightful thought. As much as I would prefer to use a pre-digital sound for the comparison, though, I must reluctantly concede that the likening to a smoke alarm's low-battery alert is more accurate.

Adult midwife toads hunt at night. During the day, they avoid desiccation not by submerging themselves in water but instead by hiding under objects, such as plants pots, or in a burrow in the earth. So my wife was right when she said that the sound was coming from the soil.

The species is native to western Europe but an alien in Britain. Following their accidental introduction over a century ago—via, it is thought, a consignment of imported plants—midwife toads have become established in various locations, through a combination of human-facilitated spread within the country and further colonization events. Before the species emerged as the solution to my bifold mystery, I knew of its occurrence in Britain but not of its presence in my county of residence. The discovery was thus a most wonderful surprise. And, happily, there is no indication that this life form displaces or otherwise threatens the presence of any native species.

Figure 9.1: A midwife toad in the garden (note the duckweed behind the left eye: it is not difficult to see how this aquatic plant might jump from pond to pond).

Midwife toads have a preference for habitat with lots of stony ground, numerous places to hide, loose soil to dig into, and a permanent water body. Our back garden satisfies all of these criteria. Through the work that we carried out in the early years, we unknowingly forged an ideal place for a species that was not present at the time. While no photo of the entire garden is included in the current work (a picture could undo many thousands of words), I have been asked to supply such an image for use in an upcoming book on mammals, reptiles, and amphibians as an example of good midwife toad habitat.

I am truly thrilled that midwife toads have become established in the garden. I hardly ever see an adult, but their calls, which started as a mystery, have become a dependable source of joy. Without doubt, they are the species, among all the many in the garden, that add the most to my quality of life. Before they arrived, the soundscape of summer evenings, once the always-noisy swifts had finished their airborne foraging, was all too dominated by the moans and groans of vehicles on the road and planes overhead. Only occasionally would a wild voice, such as the barking of a fox, temporarily wrestle control away from the unnatural. Now the evenings belong to non-humans once more. This is not to the liking of everyone: one local resident, for instance, wants the population to be eradicated. For me, though, there is something deeply calming about drifting into sleep while listening to a real-time assurance of life's vibrancy. ●

Chapter 10: Echoes and expectancies

A whiff of the universe makes us dream of worlds we have never seen, recalls in a flash entire epochs of our dearest experience.

Helen Keller, from her 1910 book *The World I Live In*

I am not quite done with the wild strawberry. Earlier, I described several reasons why this plant's existence in the garden gives me great pleasure. Now I will mention one more: Locked into every bite of its succulent sweet flesh, for me, are the echoes of an Alpine meadow in France's *parc national des Écrins*. I camped in this national park with my wife, years ago, before we were married, and on one of our days there we hiked from the valley floor up through the dense coniferous forest, with our goal a waterfall. Emerging above the treeline we found ourselves in a meadow so full of life that it took some time to adjust to just what we were walking through. Every square inch exuded majesty.

Hungry from the climb up to this place of paradox—boasting, at once, impossible beauty and exhilarating reality—we gorged bear-like on the small, abundant fruits of the wild strawberry. This fuelled our final ascent to the tiered cascade of the waterfall.

There we looked out over a rare Alpine valley whose aesthetics and ecology had not been trashed by skiing infrastructure. On the way back, we made time for a little more strawberrying before plunging back under the treeline and descending towards our campsite, where there would be a night of stove cooking and river-cooled beer. The surest route back into this heavenly reminiscence is via a bite of the achene-studded flesh of that divine fruit. I think it is significant that I did not need to be conscious of the forming of this sensory memory. Humans have a primal instinct for such things, one that stood us in good stead at a time before supermarkets scarred the Earth's surface.

More potent still than taste-triggered echoes are recollections stirred by a pleasure-giving aroma. One of several plants native to the Mediterranean region that grows in our garden is a daisy with the scientific name *Helichrysum italicum*. This plant has narrow sage-grey leaves and inflorescences of numerous small, canary-yellow, composite flowers. Its aroma, which is captured in its common name— the curry plant—sends me back to a particular day during a trip to the *Cévennes* region of southern France. My wife and I (now long married) were holidaying as paying guests with an English couple who had retired to the tranquillity of rural France. They lived in an old isolated house that was tucked into one of countless ripples in the landscape, and the surrounding estate was a haven for wildlife of all kinds. On meeting them on our arrival, I could not think of any better word to describe their property and landholding than *paradise*. I had clearly said the right thing: soon we were sharing a bottle of local organic *rosé* with them. I explained that my idea of paradise (like that described by Ed Abbey in *Desert Solitaire*), encompasses weeds, wildness, large lizards, and other unloved creatures, from flies to scorpions. Right again! A second bottle was soon opened.

It was difficult to bring ourselves to leave the bounds of paradise during our stay, but on one of the days, taking the advice of the ever-helpful owners, we walked up a wide forestry track that wound its way up the hill above them. The gravel track was lined by a variety of herbaceous plants, with throngs of alien and native species thriving together. I stopped at every curry plant that we passed because their flower heads were unfailingly crowded with greedily feeding insects. Also, I had myself become hooked on the plant's gently spicy aroma.

The members of one family of insects in particular, the Rhopalid bugs, seemed to me to be fixated with this species. Out of curiosity, once home, we bought a curry plant from our local garden centre to further enrich the backyard's denizens. At the time of writing, it is close to coming into flower, and so I will soon know if it has the same allure in Britain as it does in the quiet, biodiverse hills of the *Cévennes*. By this point, the height of the summer, the garden will be a heaving tangle of knapweed, teasels, trefoils, and bedstraws, while small tortoiseshell and comma butterflies will be dancing between the tops of the spindly, sky-grabbing verbenas.

In the meantime, there is another fusing of insect and plant that invigorates memories of trips taken. The connection is one that I described earlier, the feeding on rosemary by its eponymous beetles (see Figure 10.1), and it transports me back to a stay in an old farmhouse set in the peace of *le Lot*, another region of southern France. The farmhouse is surrounded by land that was previously used for commercial growing of lavender; over the past few decades,

Figure 10.1: A rosemary beetle on the garden's rosemary bush.

though, it has been converted into a wildlife refuge. The building sits within a meadow of stunning botanical diversity, and the meadow, in turn, is hugged by a horseshoe of steeply rising scrubland. Hunting is banned across the estate, and life thrives there.

In the old farmhouse's herb garden, there is a rosemary bush and on it there feed the beetles. Additionally, to the side of the steps that lead up to the main entrance of the property, there grows a large lavender plant, a reminder of the land's recent history, and the beetles have a taste for that also.

Sounds, too, can spark these metaphorical echoes. Out in the backyard, the shrieking whistle from a red kite wheeling in the sky above can send me to a canyon in the arid foothills of the Spanish Pyrenees, where this species surfs the thermals with eagles and vultures. The ruddy-ochre brickwork of two lines of terraced houses mimic the gorge's sandstone cliffs, while the exuberant swifts, slicing the air in exquisite arcs, and the local pigeons, hugging the roofs with characteristic stubbornness, between them offer a fair approximation of her crag martins.

And then, of course, there are the sounds of the midwife toads. During a rain shower on a warm day, as I hear these alien amphibians sing while I suck in the Mediterranean scent of the rosemary bush and the curry plant, the evocation peaks in vigour. Suddenly, I am not just recalling trips that I have taken but thinking of explorations to come. Soon, I will roam the wild herbscapes of southern France once more. The echoes have become expectancies.

I will close with a final example of an echo, and one that I hope will illustrate how my desire to spend time with other living beings extends to those of my own species. Each May, a cluster of yellow irises shoots up in one corner of the garden. Among the garden's ragtag assortment of street-savvy wild flowers and sprouting saplings, this plant's short-lived inflorescences are conspicuous in their elegance. In the traditional Japanese concept of *wabi-sabi*, beauty emerges from imperfection and transience. The irises'

ephemeral and out-of-place gracefulness is what bestows this on our backyard.

Yellow irises are a favourite plant of a guest who visited us with her husband one May, when the flowers were peaking in their poise and finesse. My wife and I bonded with the visiting couple over a mutual personal quality—introversion, as it happens—and our conversations flourished from there. Now, in the brief appearance of the irises' yellow splendour each year, we are reminded of their visit and the wonder-filled time that we spent together. ●

Chapter 11: Travels from a garden chair

A man could be a lover and defender of the wilderness without ever in his lifetime leaving the boundaries of asphalt, powerlines, and right-angled surfaces. We need wilderness whether or not we ever set foot in it. We need a refuge even though we may never need to go there. I may never in my life get to Alaska, for example, but I am grateful that it's there.

Ed Abbey, from *Desert Solitaire*

There was a swirling mass of water that lived in a quiet pond
It asked permission from its master to visit the lands beyond
And its master allowed it to fly
So the wind swept the whirlpool across the sky

Lyrics from the Meat Puppets song Whirlpool (1991)

As an avid appreciator of all alliteration—even if executed excessively—I eagerly advanced an idea entitled 'armchair ecotourism' in an article honouring an exceptional author, Ed Abbey. (*Overindulgent?* Okay. Ending it imminently...)

The above alliteration was an attempt, finishing forthwith, to capture the essence of a natural phenomenon that is missing from the garden. Its absence did not stop me writing about it in this book; nor has it prevented visits from grey wagtails, who are rarely apart from this thing. What I am talking about are rivers; and the essence to which I refer is the sensation of unendingness that one experiences in their company. I describe here an attempt to sate my wild-river craving from the confines of a suburban backyard with a small pond. "He who hears the rippling of rivers in these degenerate days," wrote Henry Thoreau, "will not utterly despair."

My thesis in the article on armchair ecotourism was two-fold. The first part was that anyone interested in the goals of ecotourism should strive to limit their enjoyment of at least some places to enjoyment-from-afar. This is something that can be achieved via the following steps. One: find a book that vividly describes, or is simply set in, the place in question—perhaps one that has been written by a favoured author. Two: be transported there by the words. Three: donate money to support the place's protection.

Why do I suggest this at all? Most significantly, I believe that nature-lovers who are fortunate enough to have the wealth for travel must show their love of the Earth through a restraint on long-distance trips. We know that the small harm caused by each flight adds up to gargantuan damage. And, in societies transitioning away from high-density fuels, as ours will have to, casual flying will become infeasible. This means that we cannot rely on conservation efforts being propped up in the long term by ecotourists visiting from afar. That is to say, the international conservation movement must strive to find ways to help local people support local biodiversity—benefitting from globalized aid-giving but not a globalized travel economy.

In the article, I gave an example of a trip that I took from my armchair to the desert south of Arizona, piloted by Ed Abbey and his book *Cactus Country*. Part of my reluctance to travel there, I explained, was that "I'd be exerting ecological pressure on an ecosystem from which it would be unfair to expect support for large numbers of non-desert humans." This remark exemplifies the fear, described back in Chapter 1, of harming somewhere by visiting it.

The second part of the article's thesis was that Ed Abbey's work is best enjoyed when accompanied by a mug of the burnt-black coffee that he so often wove into his writing. This proved to aid my exploration of his cactus country, which was a journey that I closed with a donation to the Arizona Wilderness Coalition. This act consummated the connection that had formed between me in the UK and those desert wildlands to the north of Mexico.

Now, I am going to travel again with Mr Abbey through the desert south-west of the United States. This time, I will be journeying down a distant river, and a great one at that: the Colorado (in the early 1960s). I will be replacing the armchair with a folding seat in the garden. Thus, in addition to an old copy of *Desert Solitaire* (with yellowed pages, torn cover, and other signs of a well-read life), I am going to require heavy-duty headphones here—and equally robust music. This is for suppressing the almost-inevitable competition for my attention from angle grinders and electric saws. Abbey might have recommended a soundtrack by his beloved Bach. I have opted, instead, for something more contemporary and more local to the river that I will be floating down: an album titled Forbidden Places by the Meat Puppets. This band hails from Phoenix, Arizona, a city whose water supply is partially drawn from the Colorado, via a lengthy diverting canal.

The third thing that I will need here is coffee. The 'lockdown' of spring 2020 has cut me off from my regular supply of smoky beans, and so I will be sipping from an alternative that would, I imagine, have been too fruity for Abbey's liking when making his river-water brew. In other words, the beans are not liquorice black. Given that the wild canyon through which Abbey floated will be impersonated by the brick walls of two rows of terraced houses, this discrepancy should be a minor concern only.

And, so, with the seat unfolded, the coffee cranked and bled, the headphones cupping my ears, and *Desert Solitaire* open at the start of the chapter titled 'Down the river', I am ready to enter Abbey's red-walled, roofless cathedral. I will reflect on the experience below, once I emerge from a week of drifting down the river that cuts through it, in the company of hoodoo-voiced great horned owls, canyon wrens tinkling "like little silver bells falling across a glockenspiel," and lizards "palpitating on the rocks."

Every time that I study that chapter of *Desert Solitaire*—this is the seventh occasion, or is it the ninth?—different things leap out at me as being of special significance in that fifty-seven-page moment. The first jumping words this time describe Abbey's observation, as he and his river partner are pushing off, that they are craving "dual solitude" in the watery wilderness ahead of them not out of a misanthropic desire for separation from others. Rather, they are seeking to renew their affection for themselves "and the human kind in general by a temporary, legal separation from the mass." This is how I feel when I encase my ears, and the spongy mass that sits between them, in headphones.

Some people may cherish humanity red in truth and flaw. My own outlook is not as rosy as that: I find myself hiding from harsh sounds, cowering when encounters tend to the chaotic, and angering easily, for instance, at unjust behaviours. But I do not think that I love the human species any less for this. I hold humans dear for being humans, as I do bugs, say, for being bugs. I also love humans for those things that bugs cannot share with me: laughter, friendship, and kindness.

Relatedly, the next part of the prose that leaps up, like an ember floating up above a camp-fire, is Abbey's description of the *silence* of his surrounds, "meaning here not the total absence of sounds, for the river and its canyons are bright with native music—but rather the total absence of confusion and clamor." *Amen* to that.

Then, while Abbey is making a lone exploration of a side canyon on foot, I have a morbid thought. What if Abbey falls and breaks his neck? What if he dies then, in the early 1960s? What if those rough notes that he made a few years earlier while working as a ranger at Arches National Monument had remained unpublished?

It soon emerges that the potential for a fatal fall is not the only hazard on the trip. During another terrestrial exploration, Abbey nearly cooks himself by means of an accidentally started brush fire (reading this, I send some coffee down the wrong chute and half-choke). *Be careful, Ed,* I plead. *You've got to get out of this in good enough shape to mould those rough notes from Arches into a book—this book I'm holding, in fact.*

And then the culminating question: without the publication of *Desert Solitaire,* would the world be different? My thoughts on this are as follows. Were it the case that Albert Einstein had not been born, a special theory of relativity would still have been postulated at some point. But had Abbey died on that trip down the Colorado, *Desert Solitaire* would have remained just rough notes in the effects of a relatively obscure novelist. This is true in the same trivial sense that any work of literature would not have been produced if the author had died before they got to writing it. But I mean something more by it than that. *Desert Solitaire* was like a boulder falling from the top of a canyon wall into society's current—a boulder so large that only Ed could push it—and its ripples are still radiating outwards more than half a century later. Without Abbey's fiery love letter to the planet's surviving wildness, activism and care for the Earth would not be what they are today.

In addition to these excursions down novel side canyons of my own making, this reading of 'Down the river' has delivered all the usual pleasures of vividly described geology and natural history, abrupt philosophizing, contagious joy, well-expressed anger—and the sense of a journey taken. Having completed the trip, I am ready to make a donation. Here, however, I encounter a problem. Last time, I sealed the episode of ecotourism with a donation to a charity working to preserve the landscapes to which Abbey had transported me. But I cannot do the same for the canyon described in 'Down the river'. There is no charity working to achieve this. Why would there be? The twisting biogeology that Abbey journeyed through now sits at the bottom of an artificial reservoir, Lake Powell, its water held in place by the Glen Canyon Dam. The river no longer runs wild. Its side canyons of wonder have become forbidden places. When I said a 'distant' river, I meant one removed both in space and in time.

Instead, I make a donation to the campaign known as Save the Blue Heart of Europe, which is working to prevent the further damming of remaining wild rivers in the Balkan Peninsula. The ripples from the boulder radiate a little further.

Abbey's river trip was made shortly before the Glen Canyon Dam was completed. He and his companion seized the soon-to-disappear opportunity to experience the river in her wild state, and to discover her secrets, before the rising of the artificial reservoir began (an imminent damming is also the over-riding motivation for the trip down the fictional Cahulawassee River in the novel and film *Deliverance*).

One of the more striking marks of our culture to distant generations will surely be our accounts of beautiful places that were later destroyed, and creatures that were allowed to go extinct. These future people may have their work cut out trying to reconcile such accounts with our contemporaneous reports that celebrate the cause of destruction and loss—namely, the ideology of unceasingly growing the human enterprise.

Abbey's was a deliberate act of recording a wild river on the verge of being extinguished. So many other records of beauty that we will pass down, however, will not have been written for this reason. Their writers might not have even dreamt that their loss could be possible, or that destructive forces loomed so large on the horizon. ◉

Chapter 12:
Green-letter days

Another glorious day, the air as delicious to the lungs as nectar to the tongue...

John Muir, from *My First Summer in the Sierra*

If the theme of travel that ran through the preceding pair of chapters suggested to you a wanderlust on my part—perhaps, even, a fatigue with the garden—let me reassure you that the garden has captivated me throughout the writing of this book. Indeed, it has been the setting for several celebrations, three of which I will describe in this chapter.

Some of the special occasions in the garden occur on dates that cannot be known with precision in advance. This category includes, for instance: the dusk that draws the first bat out from hibernation, twisting into the coming night with impossible grace; and the day that brings home the vanguard of the swifts returning from Africa; and the hour in which the ox-eye daisies' inaugural inflorescence opens. Then there are special dates that are anchored to natural phenomena, such as the equinoxes and solstices. In addition, there are some dates that are entirely human in their nature. Of the celebrations that I report here, one pivots on a natural phenomenon:

the earliest dawn of the year. The other two are based on human occurrences. The first of these is a conjoined marking of the 182nd anniversary of John Muir's birth (on 21st April, or John Muir Day) and the 50th Earth Day (on 22nd April), this latter occasion being a global event for demonstrating support for planetary conservation. And the second is International Dawn Chorus Day, which takes place on the earliest Sunday in May each year.

Late evenings and early mornings are the periods within the bounds of my waking when other humans are quietest; these times thus offer the best opportunity for enjoying a deep connection with the rest of nature in the suburbs. The three celebrations take advantage of these windows. I describe each of the occasions below, in the order in which they happened.

John Muir Day and Earth Day 50 (21st–22nd April)

Compared with clinging to the slender and supple top of a one-hundred-foot tall Douglas fir during a gale—an experience that John Muir described in *The Mountains of California*—camping out in one's backyard on a mild, rainless night could hardly be considered adventurous. But, under 'lockdown' conditions, it was the best way I could think of to honour the spirit of the great wilderness defender. And so here I am, with midnight approaching, flat on my back in the garden, staring up at a cloudless sky and listening to the lush Mediterraneoid soundscape of conversing midwife toads. I say that midnight is nearing. I have been out here since 11pm, and my judgement that not quite an hour has passed is a vague one, based as it is on the Plough's rotation in the sky.

The sounds of the toads are particularly absorbing during the spring in which this camp-out is taking place. Ordinarily, the sky would be roaring fitfully with the traffic of a nearby airport, but flights are temporarily on hold. There are also noticeably fewer cars on the road. In fact, I am conscious of only one incursion of the technosphere into my wild reverie. There are a couple of branches of the cherry tree that arch over the fence. The trembling of their foliage, with the merest breath of wind, triggers a motion sensor that switches on a light in the neighbour's garden. Then, the circuit counts to five and the light flicks off. As soon as the air stirs again, the loop begins once more. This tethering of such an agreeable natural phenomenon as a gently pulsating breeze to a technological after-effect quickly becomes niggling. Fortunately, I can take my glasses off and shut my eyes, while still enjoying the soft crests of the zephyr—and the ripples of amphibian music. (The sleeping bag that I am in, and the mat on which it lies, could also, I suppose, be considered incursions of the technosphere. But when these two items are at their most helpful is when they are not noticed: this is my ideal kind of technology.)

With my eyes now closed, a thought strikes me about the connection of breeze to artificial light. While an annoyance for me, John Muir might, himself, have found something satisfying in its workings. This man of diverse talents devoted significant energy in his early life to mechanical inventions, before he was driven away from the world of machinery by an accident in which he temporarily lost his sight. Among his creations was an alarm-clock device that slid him out of bed at his chosen hour while simultaneously lighting a lamp.

The breeze is exerting another effect via the cherry, this one entirely natural. Its every breath unhitches an array of petals from the tree's flowers. Once detached, they float down, in the starlight, like confetti for my celebration. Yet they are not *for me*: their principal work has been on behalf of the flowers, guiding in potential pollinators. More generally—and talking now of a tree as a metaphor for life's organization—humans are not an apex but merely a twig at the end of a branch that is much like any other.

The notion that humans are exceptional among Earthly beings is one that John Muir was among the first modern Western thinkers to challenge, as is evidenced by a journal entry—later published in *A Thousand-Mile Walk to the Gulf*—that he made in 1867, when he was twenty-nine years old. In this entry, Muir, a Christian raised in strict Protestant tradition, challenged those who promoted the orthodoxy of the Great Chain of Being, which is a hierarchical organization of the universe in which humans are granted supremacy over all other mortal beings:

Now, it never seems to occur to these far-seeing teachers that Nature's object in making animals and plants might possibly be first of all the happiness of each one of them, not the creation of all for the happiness of one. Why should man value himself as more than a small part of the one great unit of creation?

As "the prevailing model in Western history," writes Eileen Crist, the Great Chain folds "the beliefs of human superiority and entitlement into a single cosmological package." Despite the *biological* challenge levelled against this model by Alfred Russel Wallace and Charles Darwin in the theory of evolution by natural selection, as well as the *moral* challenge presented by Muir and many others since, the cosmology of the Great Chain retains much of its potency of influence to this day. On this, Crist notes:

> The Great Chain of Being with man at the top is everywhere: it is the "dark matter" permeating the world. Modernity did not abandon the Great Chain but gave it a new twist.

I re-open my eyes, put my glasses back on, stare up again at the Plough, and quickly locate the great aid to navigation in times of darkness that is the Pole Star. Staring through over four-hundred light-years of space, I am at once reassured of the fragility of the notion of *Homo sapiens* as supreme beings. My celebration of John Muir Day has gone well, and my thoughts turn, now, to another challenger of human exceptionalism, Aldo Leopold, who died on this same date, in 1948, while fighting a wild fire on a neighbour's property. (The date also adds another year to my own tally, but this—except, perhaps, to my parents—is of minuscule significance in comparison.)

Sometime later, I drift off. I had hoped to awake well before sunrise for a prime viewing of the Lyrids meteor shower, a cyclical phenomenon that peaks each year around John Muir Day. But I sleep longer than this, and by the time that I stir I can already taste dawn in the air. So, instead, I content myself with listening to the avian chorus that heralds the 50th Earth Day. As I do this, a memory crystallizes of a dream that I have just had. It is a common one for me: I am bounding through a landscape on all fours. I wonder if Wallace or Darwin or Leopold or Muir were ever inspired by such a fantasy.

The dawn chorus is a highlight for me of any occasion on which I sleep outside. Similarly, early-morning bird sightings easily become etched on my mind like wondrous works of art. On a two-day walking trip around a wild curve of the Essex coastline, a friend and I were treated to an unforgettable avocet fly-by as we broke our fast on the second morning. We were camping wild and we exercised discreteness in every way that we could. Mirroring a desire expressed by Robert Louis Stevenson in *Travels with a Donkey in the Cévennes*, we did not wish to "advertise [our] intention of camping out to every curious passer-by." Thus, we travelled with a cover story for anyone whom we should meet, to explain the backpacks, and we lit no camp-fires. In fact, we never light these. This abstention, coupled with itinerant and obsessive litter-picking, helps us surpass the leave-no-trace ideal in these stealth-camping experiences.

On another of our wild-camping trips, this same friend and I slept in the woods under a tarpaulin, with an unobscured view of the bases of the trees all around us. And so it was birds, again, who captivated us as we slowly awoke to the new day: We spent the first two post-dawn hours watching treecreepers deftly remove insects from the craggy surface of the trunks.

More recently, during a 'trial run' in the backyard for my John Muir Day camp-out, a heron sailed above my head as I sipped a morning brew. It was only the second occasion on which I had seen a member of this majestic species come so close to the garden.

I wonder what surprises the present morning might bring… I drift off again and the next time I awake it is well past sunrise. The avian chatter has subsided and a different sound, coming from the nearby cat-mint, is dominant. What I can hear is the buzzing of hairy-footed flower bees. It is still an hour or more before the sunlight will hit the garden, but these insects are already busy with the day's chores.

As for an unexpected sighting, it turns out that, on this particular morning, there is to be nothing out of the ordinary. I find myself perfectly content, however, with the everyday beauty of the matrix that nourishes me. A wood pigeon perches serenely under the apex of a nearby cypress, receiving the first rays of light. A robin, taking an inaugural dip in the pond for the day, flutters joyfully. A high-spirited magpie enters the stage.

International Dawn Chorus Day (3rd May)

I sleep inside and set an alarm for 4am, although it turns out that I did not need to. I am awoken a couple of minutes before the designated hour by the barking of foxes, who are prowling the streets on this cool, clear morning. Outside, a hint of dawn is apparent in the lowest part of the sky that I can see. The Earthly horizon, something lacking from a suburban existence, is outside my field of view.

I descend the stairs and put on a pot of tea. The birds have started to gently probe the coming lightness from the tree-lined edge of a park, a couple of streets away. This park is the part of Marston Nine Acre Field land that was spared conversion to housing during the construction of Fleetville, which I described in Chapter 2.

My wife slowly makes her way down to join me, and we sit outside, clutching warm mugs. With forty-five minutes having passed since I awoke, and another forty-five to go before sunrise, the individual strains and refrains have multiplied and merged into a chorus. The sound still feels distant, though, having the quality of an ensemble tuning up in a closed room down a corridor. Then, the clear and plaintive melody of a mistle thrush begins from the top of a nearby tree. Soon, other birds join in from the surrounding gardens and it becomes difficult to pick out the part of any one bird. Right here, in an unremarkable part of a small city, an awe-inspiring and entirely absorbing natural phenomenon is taking place. And no monstrous machines pass overhead to break the spell.

By the time that sunrise comes—a somewhat arbitrary event in the horizonless suburbs—the chorus has eased and individual voices are clear once more. The spellbinding start to the day has drawn to a close.

Earliest dawn (17th June)

The earliest dawn of the year occurs not on the summer solstice but a few days before. For the coming of this new day, I decide not to rise early but to stay up in its anticipation. And so here I am, peering out over the garden at 9.30pm on 16th June, sipping a strong caffeinated tea. A tough spring is coming to an end.

In England, May was not only the driest documented instance of the month but also the sunniest ever calendar month on record. All told, during the preceding seven weeks, there has been only one really good drenching from the skies. Mercifully, rain has been forecast with a high likelihood tonight. A deep thirst that is cresting in the garden and its creatures may at last be slaked.

I put the tea down and step outside. Amphibious forms are cautiously leaving the safety of the pond, perhaps sensing, like I am, that rain is imminent. The frogs—possibly out of a desire for exclusive stamping grounds, or maybe just by random forces—radiate out across the garden, on purposeful courses, like spokes from a hub. Above me, the swifts pick a few last morsels out of the day's fading light, as other birds fly across towards their roosts. In a nearby garden, the intonation of a song thrush, who is issuing final thoughts for the evening, remains clear above the rising chorus of midwife toads. Around me, moths bounce through the air on their erratic paths, which presumably serve them well in evading bats. And, right under my nose, on a ribwort plantain flower head, several shieldbug nymphs seem to be huddling into a group for the night (see Figure 12.1).

I leave the frogs to their hunting and head back inside to attend to a couple of things. An hour and a half later, when I next emerge, the predicted rain has begun to fall, and the night air is sweet on the tongue and full of promise. I carefully pick a path using the light of a dim torch, avoiding the amphibians and their mollusc prey. Life is everywhere. I cannot recall a time when I have seen more frogs out in the garden, nor one when the midwife toads have been rejoicing so vociferously. Getting a little greedy, I wonder if I might be lucky enough to see one of these secretive Mediterranean amphibians tonight. I return to the French windows that lead into the kitchen, switching off the torch so that I can spend a couple of minutes in darkness, under the falling rain, before heading back in.

Figure 12.1: Common green shieldbug nymphs
on a ribwort plantain flower head.

When I next venture out into the backyard, it is half past midnight, with sunrise still four hours away. The rain has stopped, the stars are out, and it is noticeably cooler. There are more slugs and fewer frogs on the paving stones, compared with an hour and a half earlier.

A small creature catches my eye as I pass the weak beam of the torch around the edge of the pond. *Could it be that elusive amphibian?* I make a closer inspection and am thrilled to confirm that I am looking at a midwife toad. The creature is heading away from the water. Midwife toads, as I understand it, generally visit water bodies only when they have eggs on their back. This is for one of two reasons: to keep the eggs moist as they develop; or to allow the tadpoles to hatch, once ready, into the water. The toad in front of me, like the small number whom I've seen before, is not carrying eggs. Is this, then, I wonder, a male who has just completed the delivery of his newly hatched children?

I leave the garden in darkness for a further ninety minutes and return with my torch at 2am. This time, a brief survey of the pond catches activity in the water, and I carefully shuffle round to get closer.

I cannot believe what I am watching.

For the first time in my life, I am looking at a midwife toad with eggs twisted round his back legs. Moreover, I can see that the tadpoles are emerging. This is as good as it gets. Overwhelmed with joy, and humbled by my insignificance, I leave him to finish his act of delivery and retreat into the house.

I am riding a high from what I have just seen, but there are two and a half hours still to go till sunrise. I realize then that the garden has already given me more pleasure than I had any right to hope for during a single night, and I decide that I do not need to see the dawn. Also, I am pretty bloody tired.

I turn in and listen to the music of the midwife toads from bed, through an open window. Tonight, there is no place that I would rather be.

Postscript: A trip to Dunbar

What was I saying about a wanderlust?

A few months after the above celebrations, I was lucky enough to be able to strengthen my connection with John Muir by taking a three-day trip to Dunbar, his hometown, on the east coast of Scotland. The visit began with a deeply moving tour of the museum that is dedicated to his life and work. This museum is situated on Dunbar's high street, in the house where Muir was born. Soon after his birth, his family moved into the much larger residence next door, and it was in this house that he spent the rest of his childhood up to the point when, aged eleven, he emigrated with his family to the States. Muir, who was destined to be a great mountaineer, used to scale the tall wall at the back of this property's large rear garden to escape into the countryside. At the time of my visit, the wall had been torn down to allow developers in to begin work on a small block of flats in the garden. As sad—and as blackly apt for the modern age—as this development is, it did give me the opportunity to poke my nose into Muir's boyhood backyard.

After this, I spent much of the rest of my time in Dunbar wandering along the sea front, dodging the missiles being launched by golfers on the town's two links, marvelling at the coastline's astonishing volcanic geology (see Figure 12.2), losing time in the crashing of waves against the ruins of the town's harbour castle, and exploring the very same limpet- and anemone-rich rockpools that so enthralled Muir as a boy. It is not hard to see how a life-curious child would have fallen in love with nature, and her wild forces, growing up in nineteenth-century Dunbar.

The trip also gave me cause to muse further on that story I mentioned at the beginning of this chapter, where Muir climbed to the apex of a tall Douglas fir to experience the full force of a gale. Although I do not generally feel the wind or cold like most people I know do (a consequence, no doubt, of my wife and I under-heating our home), in my three days exploring Dunbar I was rarely out of a fleece and stormproof shell. The wind is fierce on the coastline there. Many of the locals, though, seemed content in rather less substantial clothing than that which I was wearing. Some especially hardy souls chose to cover their top half with nothing more than a T-shirt.

I wonder whether Muir developed a wind tolerance during his childhood years on the coast and thus—like a chilli fiend who cannot satisfy a desire for heat without the spiciest pepper—needed a truly tempestuous wind to sate his own craving. And perhaps, then, he climbed the fir in the storm simply because he was homesick. ⬡

Figure 12.2: Rocks on Dunbar's coastline.

Part four

---◇---

Gazing nervously forward

Chapter 13:
The future of
the garden

And you show your heart
And you show your grace, so radical
The world is sleeping
With a monster most mechanical

Lyrics from the Sea Within song *The Void* (2018)

We must regain control
Or there'll be nothing left to save
The harmony of nature
Twisted into discordance
Left to die in the aftermath
Of their destructive sightlessness
Time is running
Time is running
Time is running
Time is running out

Lyrics from the Earth Crisis song *Inherit the Wasteland* (1995)

I t is said, by technophiles, that we (people living in wealthier countries) are living during the greatest time the world has ever known. Supermarket shelves brim with exotic produce all year round. Mobile phones facilitate a constant interconnectivity of social groups. Cooling and heating units control our environment when we are in buildings and in vehicles, regardless of the external conditions. Fibre-optic cables bring us unlimited high-definition entertainment. *Et cetera. Et cetera.* In short, humans have overcome the 'challenges' to happiness imposed by a temporary lack of access to particular food items (otherwise known as seasonality), a temporary loss of contact with friends and family (alone time), a temporary reduction in ambient comfort (appreciation by contrast), and a temporary wait for something entertaining (anticipation). Working in tandem with the tendency for large corporations to thrive at the expense of individual artisans and small enterprises, developments like these have all contributed to a homogenization of human life.

Now, it is possible, if one so wishes, to partially negate this homogenization. For instance, I can protest against unseasonal, exotic produce as a consumer by not buying it. I can choose to only turn on my own mobile phone (a device that was unwanted by its first owner and was passed on to me) at limited times, such as when meeting someone. I can spend as much time as possible outdoors, travelling between places on foot where I can, and allow my home to gently buffer weather extremes rather than obliterating them. And I can limit my access to streaming services. I know that people often think that I am weird in how I choose to live my life, and sometimes even find me difficult. But I have to be like this, because I know that change is needed, and I believe that the roots of change gain their firmest grip in the humus of individual actions.

But the homogenization of life as a human is far from being the main issue with the rampant march of our technological, progress-driven culture. The overwhelming problem lies in the externalities of progress: the unaccounted-for and so-often-ignored casualties of human economic growth. Among these externalities are the whole-sale destruction of biotically rich habitats, the toxification of water through mining operations, the destabilization of the climate, the poisoning of wild plants and insects, the torture suffered by domesticated animals in industrial agriculture, and the plummeting of wild populations in seas, rivers, and, lakes. All of these things are a direct result of technological progress. All of these things are reasons why the human enterprise, as currently playing out, is not a cause for technophilic celebration but, to put it frankly, a mortifying disgrace.

I readily acknowledge that humans are capable of amazing ingenuity, and that at least some of it is beneficial for non-humans, at least in mopping up the mess that it has so often caused. Furthermore, I would be a terrible hypocrite to try to deny that I have personally benefitted from many technological developments. Without penicillin, for example, I would quite probably have died, at the age of four, from a burst appendix and the complication of peritonitis (both things were picked up late by sceptical doctors, who left me to stew in the waiting room for the best part of a day as they attended to routine matters, despite the insistence of my parents that something really was not right with me).

But my protest is not against human ingenuity *per se*. Rather, I am challenging the hubris of human supremacy that underlies run-away 'progress' and that is, I believe, the unspoken mantra of technophilia. I am skewering that most sacred of cows in 'free world' politics: growth at any cost.

So what do I propose instead? What is needed, I feel, is not a rigid anti-technology stance, but, instead, a desire to critically appraise developments in a way that fully and fairly accounts for externalities within the true economy of life on Earth. I am not talking about coming up with fancy tricks that enable us to put a dollar sign in front of nature. The Earth's currency is the flourishing of life for life's sake—and this is a value that cannot be financialized. As the philosopher Adam Dickerson neatly puts it:

[E]conomics is no 'master discourse', within which all problems can be framed, and which legitimately has the 'last word'.

As for what an Earth-centred economics should look like, Dickerson notes:

Most crucially, it must tackle the profoundly difficult problem of how the intrinsic moral value of other-than-human nature can be embedded within economic decision making and governance.

Finally, I should note that I am not naïve: I know that my writing all of this on a page is not enough to make it happen. But if a sufficient number of people can challenge a system that, in purportedly delivering progress, is actually making the average human existence worse rather than better—while killing off life on Earth—then there is a chance for change. As long as the present system operates, though, I will fear the worst.

Just as I have concerns about life on Earth on a global scale, I am worried about the future of my backyard. With increasing demands placed on existing infrastructure by the building of ever-more houses, life in a city is, for me, growing less and less tolerable as each year passes. At some point soon, my wife and I will need to escape for good. (We are very fortunate, I know, to have a choice.)

The worst thing about leaving will be relinquishing our power to protect the garden and its denizens. I worry, for instance, that the fences will be replaced and the hedgehog holes lost. I fret that the ivy will be killed back and a vital source of autumn nectar thus eliminated. And I have a deep concern that something like the following conversation is going to take place soon after the new owners come in:

Builder: So you want to do a loft conversion? *Owners:* Yes, of course. We'd be silly not to, right? I can't believe the last owners didn't do it. We'd have had to pay a lot more if they had. *Builder:* So you're going to need a skip for all the waste it's going to make. *Owners:* There's no chance, I suppose, that you could dispose of it… you know… another way? We'd like to keep our costs down as much as possible, you see. *Builder:* Oh, is that a pond you've got in the garden? *Owners:* Yes. Why do you ask? *Builder:* Well, if you were happy to lose the pond, I could get quite a bit of the waste in there and cover it up. We could even fit some plastic grass on top of that. My brother does that, so I could get you a great deal. *Owners:* Brilliant idea. Yes to filling the pond in. Yes to the lazy lawn. Now, what else do we need to discuss…

So do we just stay? I am certainly curious to know what the garden would look like in thirty years' time, if we left it to continue on its path towards a hazel micro-woodland—which is what the squirrels have had in mind all along.

Probably, in the end, the decision will be settled by the cold, rational analysis that we can do more good with more land. But this thought will not make it any easier to say goodbye to the garden, or the many residents whose future we may well be imperilling. It will not lessen the pain of separation from our fellow Earthlings in the deep green neighbourhood. ⬢

Afterword:
A broader
horizon

As 'lockdown' restrictions were lifted after the initial wave of Covid-19 infections in England began to subside, my wife and I tentatively ventured out to a local picnic site that we had not been to in over a decade (this was before a further relaxation of restrictions permitted the trip to Dunbar described in the postscript to Chapter 12). The picnic site was created as a stop along an old railway line that has been repurposed as a dual-use cycleway and walking route. For a picnic site, it is unusually secluded, having no human settlement, or even a car park, in its vicinity. On our last visit, though, it had been heavily littered, and it felt then like it was on the cusp of becoming an informal rubbish dump.

As we neared the site on foot, for a return that had been a long time coming, I feared the worst. In fully expecting to encounter rubbish strewn everywhere, I was experiencing a heavy dose of 'topoaversion'— Glenn Albrecht's term for a reluctance to revisit a cherished place that one knows (or, in this case, strongly suspects) has undergone negative change at the hands of others. Therefore, when we arrived and found the area completely free of trash, and looking even more welcoming than it had before, it was a cause both for joy and for relief.

There were two benches at the site. One was already taken, by a cyclist enjoying a tranquil lunch, but the other was free and we eagerly claimed it. I took out a lightweight camping stove from my bag and was soon frying up a couple of pea-protein burgers and adding gherkins and other accompaniments to a pair of freshly baked bread rolls. I do not think I am exaggerating in saying that it was as pleasurable a picnic as I have ever had.

After lunch we continued to stroll along the old railway line and soon came to a junction point. Here, a footpath left the track and gently descended along the edge of a field. There was an abundance of pineappleweed where the path left the track, which might have been dangerous were if not for an even greater distraction, especially for a 'capitulator' like me. The end of a field had been left as a set-aside and was full of ox-eye daisies. I made a conservative estimate that I was staring out across more than half a million daisy flower heads, and there were countless other wild flowers too (see Figure A.1).

I was also staring out over one of the key battlegrounds for the fate of life on Earth in our time: the land that humans use for agriculture. If we are to widen the bottleneck through which we are forcing life, and if we are to soften the impending collapse that now seems inevitable for humanity, then we must free up much of the land that we are currently farming for rewilding and then manage the remainder in ways that are more ecologically sound and that place less stress on the planet's watersheds. Soil and water are life-giving ingredients over which no one species has a right to claim dominion

Figure A.1: A set-aside with half a million or more ox-eye daisy flower heads.

or a monopoly. The emerging Earth ethic demands that these things be shared. Simultaneously, key priorities in implementing an Earth ethic must be to let recover the struggling life of the Earth's oceans and freshwater systems, as well as the ravaged populations of wild terrestrial animals. So harried is the Earth's wildlife that nothing less than widespread moratoria on killing are likely to suffice, with limited exceptions for the subsistence of cultures with no decent alternatives.

Furthermore, despite what is stated in the main tenet of the currently dominant environmentalist discourse, a shift in the patterns of consumption will not, by itself, allow us to release our lethal stranglehold on the Earth. Rather, humane programmes to ease the Earth's human population downward will also be of fundamental importance here. In both of these things, the onus, I firmly believe, is on developed nations to lead the way in a great global downscaling. Furthermore, citizens of these nations will need to be ever-more demanding of their governments, because if the changes come only from the top, they will fall woefully short of what is required.

Everything points towards a choice between a significantly downscaled future for humans or very little future at all. Maybe you are already on a journey to being a part of this great Earth-revering shrinkage. If not, how would you like to join me? ●

Bibliography

Preface

Austin MH (1903) *The Land of Little Rain.* Boston, MA, USA:
    Houghton, Mifflin and Company.
Owen J (1991) *The Ecology of a Garden: The first fifteen years.*
    Cambridge, UK: Cambridge University Press.
Owen J (2010) *Wildlife of a Garden: A thirty-year study.* London, UK:
    Royal Horticultural Society.
Shepherd N (1977) *The Living Mountain.* Aberdeen, UK: Aberdeen
    University Press.

Chapter 1

Albrecht G (2019) *Earth Emotions: New words for a new world.* Ithaca,
    NY, USA: Cornell University Press.
Curry P (2017) The Ecological Citizen: An impulse of life, for life.
    The Ecological Citizen **1**: 5–9.
Gray J (2019) Entomology as an appreciation of life on a different
    scale. *Country-Side* **35**: 17–18.
Leopold A (1972) The round river – a parable. In: Leopold LB, ed.
    Round River. Oxford, UK: Oxford University Press, 158–65.
Mann P (2013) *The Disestablishment of Paradise.* London, UK:
    Gollancz.

Mortillaro N (2017) More than 15,000 scientists from 184 countries issue 'warning to humanity'. *CBC News*, 13 November.

Næss A (1973) The shallow and the deep, long-range ecology movement. A summary. *Inquiry* **16**: 95–100.

Shoard M (2000) Edgelands of promise. *Landscapes* **2**: 74–93.

Rowe S (2006) *Earth Alive: Essays on ecology*. Edmonton, AB, Canada: NeWest Press.

Thoreau HD (1863) *Excursions*. Boston, MA, USA: Ticknor and Fields.

Tolkien JRR (2004) *The Lord of the Rings* (50th Anniversary Edition). London, UK: HarperCollins.

Chapter 2

Catt J, ed (2010) *Hertfordshire Geology and History*. Welwyn Garden City, UK: Hertfordshire Natural History Society.

Charles L, Dodge J, Milliman L, and Stockley V (1981) Where you at? A bioregional quiz. *CoEvolution Quarterly* **32**(Winter): 1.

Marsh GP (1864) *Man and Nature; or, Physical Geography as Modified by Human Action*. New York, NY, USA: Charles Scribner & Co.

Monbiot G (2014) *Feral: Rewilding the land, sea and human life*. London, UK: Penguin.

Neighbour M (2012) *St Albans' Own East End. Volume 1: Outsiders*. Self-published.

Rackham O (2012) *Woodlands*. London, UK: HarperCollins.

Vera F (2000) *Grazing Ecology and Forest History*. Wallingford, UK: CABI Publishing.

William M (2003) *Deforesting the Earth: From prehistory to global crisis*. Chicago, IL, USA: University of Chicago Press.

Chapter 3

Berry W (2018) *The World-Ending Fire*. London, UK: Penguin.

Calcott A and Bull J (2007) *Ecological Footprint of British City Residents*. Godalming, UK: WWF-UK.

Davies ZG, Fuller RA, Loram A, *et al.* (2009) A national scale inventory of resource provision for biodiversity within domestic gardens. *Biological Conservation* **142**: 761–71.

Goulson D (2019) *The Garden Jungle: Or gardening to save the planet.* London, UK: Jonathan Cape.

Leopold A (1968) *A Sand County Almanac: And sketches here and there.* New York, NY, USA: Oxford University Press.

Plotica LP (2020) Politics is not enough: Individual action and the limits of institutions. *The Ecological Citizen* **4**: 37–43.

Tengö J and Bergström G (1977) Cleptoparasitism and odor mimetism in bees: Do *Nomada* males imitate the odor of *Andrena* females? *Science* **196**: 1117–19.

Chapter 4

Albrecht G (2019) *Earth Emotions: New words for a new world.* Ithaca, NY, USA: Cornell University Press.

Baker JA (2017) *The Peregrine* (50th anniversary edition). London, UK: William Collins.

Berry W (2018) *The World-Ending Fire.* London, UK: Penguin.

Colman AM (2008) *Oxford Dictionary of Psychology.* Oxford, UK: Oxford University Press.

Crist E (2019) *Abundant Earth: Toward an ecological civilization.* Chicago, IL, USA: University of Chicago Press.

Curry P (2018) *Ecological Ethics: An introduction* (updated second edition). Cambridge, UK: Polity Press.

Ehrenfeld D (1981) *The Arrogance of Humanism.* Oxford, UK: Oxford University Press.

Fossey D (1985) *Gorillas in the Mist: A remarkable story of thirteen years spent living with the greatest of the great apes.* London, UK: Penguin.

Leopold A (1968) *A Sand County Almanac: And sketches here and there.* New York, NY, USA: Oxford University Press.

Livingston JA (2007) *The John A. Livingston Reader.* Toronto, ON, Canada: McClelland & Stewart.

Muir J (1938) *John of the Mountains: The unpublished journals of John Muir* (edited by Wolfe LM). Boston, MA, USA: Houghton Mifflin.

Næss A (1973) The shallow and the deep, long-range ecology movement. A summary. *Inquiry* **16**: 95–100.

Rowe S (1990) *Home Place: Essays on ecology.* Edmonton, AB, Canada: NeWest Press.

Royal Horticultural Society (2020) *Algae, lichens, liverworts and moss on hard surfaces.* Available at https://is.gd/WEyHgK (accessed June 2020).

Smith IA (2016) *The Intrinsic Value of Endangered Species.* New York, NY, USA: Routledge.

Sobel D (1996) *Beyond Ecophobia: Reclaiming the heart in nature education.* Great Barrington, MA, USA: Orion Society.

Sylvan R (1973) Is there a need for a new, an environmental ethic? In: *Proceedings of the XII World Congress of Philosophy* (no. 1). Varna, Bulgaria: 205–10.

Tuan Y-F (1974) *Topophilia: A study of environmental perceptions, attitudes, and values.* New York, NY, USA: Columbia University Press.

Vogt B (2017) *A New Garden Ethic: Cultivating defiant compassion for an uncertain future.* Gabriola Island, BC, Canada: New Society Publishers.

Whyte I and Gray J (2020) Field guides as a gateway to appreciating more-than-human concerns. *The Ecological Citizen* **3**: 119.

Wilson EO (1984) *Biophilia.* Cambridge, MA, USA: Harvard University Press.

Wilson EO (1995) Biophilia and the conservation ethic. In: Kellert SR and Wilson EO, eds. *The Biophilia Hypothesis.* Washington, DC, USA: Island Press, 31–41.

Chapter 5

BBC Gardeners' World Magazine (2020) *Rosemary beetle: Prevent damage to your herbs by adult and juvenile rosemary beetles.* Available at https://is.gd/ZoYqPx (accessed June 2020).

Berry W (2018) *The World-Ending Fire.* London, UK: Penguin.

Crist E (2019) *Abundant Earth: Toward an ecological civilization.* Chicago, IL, USA: University of Chicago Press.

Greer JM (2009) *The Ecotechnic Future: Envisioning a post-peak world.* Gabriola Island, BC, Canada: New Society Publishers.

Mabey R (2012) *Weeds: The story of outlaw plants.* London, UK: Profile Books.

Snyder G (1990) *The Practice of the Wild.* Berkeley, CA, USA: Counterpoint.

Thoreau HD (2001) *Wild Fruits: Thoreau's rediscovered last manuscript* (Dean BP, ed). New York, NY, USA: WW Norton & Company.

Wood A (2016) *Butterflies of Hertfordshire and Middlesex*. St Albans, UK: Hertfordshire Natural History Society.

Chapter 6

Albrecht G (2019) *Earth Emotions: New words for a new world*. Ithaca, NY, USA: Cornell University Press.

Fabre JH (1979) *Insects* (Black D, ed). London, UK: Paul Elek.

Fuller RJ and Warren MS (1993) *Coppiced Woodlands: Their management for wildlife* (second edition). Peterborough, UK: Joint Nature Conservation Committee.

Gray J (2019) 'Making hay': A conditional defence on ecocentric grounds of various co-created habitats. *The Ecological Citizen* **3** (Suppl A): 43–54.

Lawrence DH (1974) *Apocalypse*. Harmondsworth, UK: Penguin Books.

Royal Horticultural Society (2020) *Enchanter's nightshade*. Available at https://is.gd/bpc6kI (accessed June 2020).

Santos Guerra A and Reyes Betancort JA (2011) Echium pininana. *IUCN Red List of Threatened Species*: e.T165250A5996251. Available at https://is.gd/C6YMky (accessed June 2020).

Tolkien JRR (2004) *The Lord of the Rings* (50th Anniversary Edition). London, UK: HarperCollins.

Chapter 7

Abbey E (1973) *Cactus Country: The world's wild places*. Amsterdam, the Netherlands: Time-Life.

Charles L, Dodge J, Milliman L, and Stockley V (1981) Where you at? A bioregional quiz. *CoEvolution Quarterly* **32**(Winter): 1.

Eckersley R (2012) Representing nature. In: Alonso S, Keane J, and Merkel W, eds. *The Future of Representative Democracy*. Cambridge, UK: Cambridge University Press, 236–57.

Gray J (2019) A spring of empathy in a barren landscape. *The Ecological Citizen* **2**: 124.

Gray J (2020) Other lives. *City Creatures Blog*, 4 February. Available at https://is.gd/sC5rEA (accessed June 2020).

Shepherd N (1977) *The Living Mountain*. Aberdeen, UK: Aberdeen University Press.

Ver Valley Society (2011) *Ver Valley Walk 1: The Source Walk*. Available at https://is.gd/PQ6ESo (accessed June 2020).

Wilson G and Lee DM (2019) Rights of rivers enter the mainstream. *The Ecological Citizen* **2**: 183–7.

Chapter 8

Goodall J (2005) *Harvest for Hope: A guide to mindful eating*. New York, NY, USA: Warner Books

Mabey R (2012) *Weeds: The story of outlaw plants*. London, UK: Profile Books.

Royal Horticultural Society (2020) Dipsacus fullonum *(common teasel)*. Available at https://is.gd/qmzNrX (accessed June 2020).

Ryan R (2015) The Undertaker Bug, *Chlamydatus evanescens* (Boheman) (Hemiptera: Miridae), denizen of urban cemeteries. *British Journal of Entomology and Natural History* **28**: 192.

Williams KS and Gilbert LE (1981) Insects as selective agents on plant vegetative morphology: egg mimicry reduces egg laying by butterflies. *Science* **212**: 467–9.

Wright J (2007) *Mushrooms* (River Cottage Handbook No. 1). London, UK: Bloomsbury Publishing.

Chapter 9

Carson R (1997) *The Sense of Wonder*. London, UK: HarperCollins

Fabre JH (1979) *Insects* (Black D, ed). London, UK: Paul Elek.

Chapter 10

Abbey E (1968) *Desert Solitaire: A season in the wilderness*. New York, NY, USA: Ballantine Books.

Keller H (1910) *The World I Live In*. New York, NY, USA: The Century Co.

Chapter 11

Abbey E (1968) *Desert Solitaire: A season in the wilderness*. New York, NY, USA: Ballantine Books.

Dickey J (1970) *Deliverance*. Boston, MA, USA: Houghton Mifflin.

Gray J (2018) Armchair ecotourism: A tribute to Edward Abbey. *The Ecological Citizen* **1**: 145–7.

Thoreau HD (1849) *A Week on the Concord and Merrimack Rivers*. Boston, MA, USA: James Munroe and Company.

Chapter 12

Crist E (2019) *Abundant Earth: Toward an ecological civilization*. Chicago, IL, USA: University of Chicago Press.

Muir J (1894) *The Mountains of California*. New York, NY, USA: The Century Co.

Muir J (1911) *My First Summer in the Sierra*. Cambridge, MA, USA: The Riverside Press.

Muir J (1916) *A Thousand-Mile Walk to the Gulf*. Boston, MA, USA: Houghton Mifflin Company.

Stevenson RL (2004) *Travels with a Donkey in the Cévennes* and *The Amateur Emigrant*. London, UK: Penguin Classics.

Chapter 13

Dickerson A (2020) Ecocentrism, economics and commensurability. *The Ecological Citizen* **3** (Suppl B): 5–11.

Afterword

Albrecht G (2019) *Earth Emotions: New words for a new world*. Ithaca, NY, USA: Cornell University Press.